For my daughter, Lynn,

Thank you for all your help sorting through thousands

of comments, reading and editing,

and for my granddaughter, Margeaux,

a well-informed woman of the 21st century!

i

WHAT YOUNG WOMEN MAY NOT KNOW:

The Sequel

CONTENTS

Introduction

One evening in 2016 I was speaking with my friend Margaret, most knowledgeable in women's affairs, at an art event in Eau Claire. Our conversation turned to women's issues and the ERA. Much to my surprise, I was astounded to learn the Equal Rights Amendment had never been ratified. It won two-thirds vote from the House of Representatives in October 1971. In March of 1972 it was approved by the Senate and sent to the states for ratification. It failed to achieve ratification by 38 or three-fourths of the states. It was never brought to a vote again!

That information rolled around in my head for nearly two years. The March on Washington D.C., after the president's 2017 inauguration happened, it all started to fall in place. I had read posts on Facebook from young women who said that their lives were perfect, they had control of their jobs, their bodies and that everything was fine and that the women in that March should have basically stayed home.

I had a bad headache for a couple of days, but when it started to subside, at midnight one night, I got out of bed and started an outline that ended up being five pages long. I decided that these young women needed to know how they came to have these perfect lives. I was pretty sure that many of them didn't have a clue.

I ended up writing an article for an "It Seems to Me" section in the Eau Claire Leader-Telegram (WI), published in February 2017. I was satisfied that I had said my piece and was able to say the main things that I wanted to say even after editing. The article was titled "What Young Women May Not Know." (*More on this later.) It was published and I assumed that would be the end of it. Silly me! The response was overwhelming. Comments 4,000+ strong were from all over the United States, Canada, Chile, Germany, Uganda, Venezuela, Russia and more. I learned more from some amazing women, young and old, and from some amazing men. Granted, there were many negative responses, 10-12%, from both men and women, but most were positive. And the stories knocked my socks off. Many raised topics that I was unaware of, like mass involuntary sterilization (funding included in Nixon's budget in 1970!) and genital mutilation that wasn't just happening in Africa. I found out what life was like for women from the late 19th century and before up to today. I will share some of the negative comments I received and why I did not address some of them.

I printed out a huge stack of all 4,000+ comments and my daughter, Lynn Dudenhoefer, and I started to categorize the comments into groups: Women's Rights, Marches, Title IX, R v W, Women's Health, LGBTQ, Education, Employment, and General Comments.

New things were appearing in the news that directly focused on some of these issues. November 18, 2018 the Eau Claire Leader-Telegram published an article titled, "Clinton voted out of curriculum" by school board in Texas. They had also planned to vote out Helen Keller. I had included a section in the article about how school boards in Texas would review curriculum for textbook publishers and edit things they didn't like. Several people had commented (*) that this did not/could not happen. This recent article is the reason I have included this information. Much to my surprise, another article followed listing the items that had been deleted and restored (Chapter VII). Yea, Technology!! Information about this, and many other women's issues, was not available to the general public before the internet!! See Chapter One.

Because newspaper articles are limited by length and edited, you cannot, as some writers suggested, go back and add or change an article. Once printed there it remains. As more and more information came in, I felt it was my obligation to print as many comments as I could so that you can see for yourself what people, men and women, younger and older, from here and afar, were saying about the past and about their lives now.

So this isn't just about young women and what they might not know, it is for everyone: male, female, young, old, and everyone in between. I hope that you might learn something from this compilation as my daughter and I did.

As an added note, I heard from some Black women that I did not address their issues, and that complaints about not being able to get a library card were not a big deal. Period! In comparison to the inequality Black women suffered, it had to seem pretty petty and I think it was partially misunderstood. The object was not the card nor the importance of the card, the object was that they could not do something so basic and so simple without a man, be it a father, husband, son or grandfather. The woman's signature alone was nothing, not even good for a damn library card! It also didn't begin to cover the struggles of LGBTQ population and hopefully I have covered more regarding that in this book, but the basis of the article was to show, mostly young women, what life was like before their lives became perfect. And how it could all change!

Sharon Weeks

What Young Women May Not Know

"It came to my attention recently, after the March on Washington, that many young women are completely satisfied with their lives right now (which isn't necessarily a bad thing.) I will refer to this as their "status quo". But first a crash course in women's history and a mention of many past marches and the influence they have had. I beg them, and you, to read on.

One thing I want to point out, as I am going to discuss women's rights from more than a hundred years ago to 2017, is what I think these young women are missing. Women's history has been basically excluded from the classroom text books in public schools. Many people are not aware that a select group of white men, a Board of Education in Texas, has been charged with the job of editing all of the history textbooks (or more) for decades. Their editing is final. (See Bill Moyers, "Messing with Textbooks," June 2012 for just one source.)

- That is the reason you probably didn't know that in the 1870's women could not own property, could not sign contracts, could not vote, file law suits, nor have their own money. Under their father's roof, he had control and that control was passed to her husband upon marriage. A woman running away from violent domestic abuse was hunted down by the law and returned to her husband as she was his property.

- From the 1840's to 1920 women fought for the vote. The struggle to gain the right to vote began nearly 200 years ago!! Attempts to vote in 1870 were turned away. The Supreme Court ruled against them in 1875. In 1916 Alice Paul formed the National Women's Party. They marched. Over 200 supporters were arrested while picketing the White House. They were beaten with clubs and thrown in prison. Some went on hunger strikes and endured forced feedings. Forty prison guards wielding clubs went on a rampage against 33 women known as The Night of Terror, 11-15-1917. See HBO movie, "Iron Jawed Angels."

- In the 1960's women fought for birth control. It was common before 1914. Gregory Pinkus developed "the pill" and it was approved by the FDA in 1960. It was illegal in many parts of the country then, you see. Margaret Sanger, a pioneer in the struggle for a woman's right to birth control in an era "when it was illegal to discuss the topic," was arrested many times for her publications and her New York City clinic (1914.) More information available at Wikipedia/Margaretsanger.

- Civil Rights Marches 1960's   People were beaten, drowned and hanged for marching. Because of the media there was more attention and the marches for these rights were better known. After the Civil War the 14th and 15th amendments adopted in 1868 & 1878

6

granted citizenship and suffrage to blacks, but not to women. A look back shows these amendments didn't help people of color then at all. A suffrage amendment to the Federal Constitution was presented to Congress since 1878 and repeatedly failed to pass. The advent of cell phone videos have given a stark look at reality and civil rights have not progressed as far as many people thought.

- 1972 Title IX is a landmark federal civil right that prohibits sex discrimination in education. Title IX is not just about sports, but is best known for that. It protects all students; The Federal government threatened to stop aid to all public schools that did not correct this.
- 1973 Roe vs. Wade made abortion legal and safe. More women stopped dying from abortions. The government is planning to stop funding for Planned Parenthood and tens of thousands of women will not only lose coverage for basic health care, but they will also no longer have access to birth control. It seems to me that no access to birth control means there will be more unwanted pregnancies. If Roe v Wade is overturned, which seems likely with the appointment of a new Supreme Court judge by this administration, there will be more women dying from abortions again.
- Gay Rights Marches Again people were beaten and killed, (think Mathew Sheppard) even when not participating in marches, but while just trying to live their lives like people of color before them. Eventually gains were made and same-sex marriage was legalized in 2015 and couples were accorded the same rights and benefits as heterosexual couples. Acceptance is at an all- time high and rising.

- Now it is 2017 and people are MARCHING. Women, their husbands, children and fathers descended upon Washington D.C. to march for women's rights. There were people marching in 57 other countries around the world! They *marched* for women all over the world, women who still make less money than men for the same work; for Muslim women and their families who fear deportation and being sent back to the terribly dangerous places they were trying so hard to flee; for Mexican families who live in fear of being deported and being torn from their children; and, to raise awareness for other people who haven't been accorded equal rights, as well as women in other countries who have few, if any, rights.

Every MARCH, every right that was fought for, that women died for, was for your "status quo," for the life you have now, that you may take for granted. Please know that every one of these rights that let you live the life you have can be erased with the swipe of a pen. Don't let all those who died, the fighting and suffering, be for naught.

Guess what? The Equal Rights Amendment did not pass!! It won the 2/3's vote from the House of Representatives in October 1971. In March of 1972 it was approved by the Senate and sent to the states for ratification. It failed to achieve ratification by 38 or ¾ of the states. It was never brought to a vote again!

Because of that rejection, sexual equality, with the exception of when it pertains to the right to vote, is not protected by the U.S. Constitution!!! However, in the late 20th century the federal government and all states have

8

passed legislation protecting women's rights. *These protections are not Amendments to the United States Constitution.* They, too, can be wiped away with the swipe of a pen especially at the state level.

Please don't be complacent and too comfortable with your life. Be aware of what has happened over the years, decades and literally, centuries, to get you here. Many people have died fighting for equal rights for themselves and others. *Women fought and died.* People MARCH to make other people aware; pay attention, please. *It is all I ask, lest you lose it all. Lest we all lose it all.*"

Chapter I

Women's Rights/History

The first section of the article goes back to the 1870's giving the history of women during that time; they could not own property, could not sign contracts, could not vote, could not file law suits nor could they have their own money. While under the father's roof he had control and that control was passed to her husband upon marriage. I wanted to give young women, who maybe didn't know about this part of women's history, the information on the past so that they might see that life has not always been as it is now in 2020. Many people did/do not know that a woman running away from violent domestic abuse was hunted down by the law and returned to her husband as she was his property.

From the 1840's to the 1920's women fought for the vote. The struggle to gain the right to vote began nearly 200 years ago. The Supreme Court ruled against them in 1875. Attempts to vote in 1879 were turned away.

In 1916 Alice Paul formed the National Women's Party. They marched! Over 200 supporters were arrested while picketing the White House. They were beaten with clubs and thrown in prison. Some went on hunger strikes and endured forced feedings. Forty prison guards wielding clubs went on a rampage against 33 women known as "The Night of Terror", 11-15-1917. See HBO movie "Iron Jawed Angels."

In 1838 Mississippi was the first state to grant women the right to hold property in their own name, with their husband's permission. In 1848 at Seneca Falls, New York, 300 women and men signed the Declaration of Sentiments, a plea for the end of discrimination against women in all spheres of society. It was drafted by Elizabeth Cady Stanton and introduced to the first women's rights convention July 19-20 in Seneca Falls. It was signed by 68 women and 32 men, with 300 in attendance.

There were so many women who commented on this article who remember that their mothers lived when women were not allowed to vote, even though the Nineteenth Amendment to the Constitution was ratified in 1920 and declared: "The right of citizens of the United States to vote shall not be denied or abridged by the United States or by any State on account of sex." Women were still denied many very basic rights well past the 1960's.

It should be noted that women in England were also struggling for the right to vote. They protested and marched, were imprisoned and force fed.

The following are some of the women, going back to the 1700's, that made it possible for us to have the life we have today:

Abigail Adams (1744-1818) was the wife of President John Adams and the mother of John Quincy Adams, who became 6th president of the United States. She served as her husband's unofficial advisor earning her the title of Mrs. President.

Abigail expressed concern about how women would be treated. In one of her many letters to her husband, she requested that he "Remember the Ladies, and be more generous and favourable to them than your ancestors. Do not put such unlimited power into the hands of the Husbands. Remember all Men would be tyrants if they could. If perticuliar care and attention is not paid to the Laidies we are determined to foment a Rebelion, and will not hold ourselves bound by any Laws in which we have no voice, or Representation." Odd spellings aside, Abigail often expressed her thoughts on political matters with her husband.[1]

Susan B. Anthony 1820-1906 was a suffragist, abolitionist, author and speaker who was the president of the National American Woman Suffrage Association. She partnered with **Elizabeth Cady Stanton** (1815-1902) to fight for women's rights. In 1872 Anthony voted illegally in the presidential election. She was arrested for the crime and fined $100, which she never paid. Anthony fought for women's rights and campaigned against slavery and alcohol. Anthony and Stanton founded the National Woman Suffrage Association giving speeches around the country to convince others to support a woman's right to vote. That right came 14 years after her death. [2]

In 1840 Elizabeth Cady Stanton_married reformer Henry Stanton (omitting "obey" from the marriage oath) and they had seven children. With Lucretia Mott and several other women, Stanton held the famous Seneca Falls Convention in July 1848. They drew up its "Declaration of Sentiments" and took the lead in proposing that women be granted the right to vote. During the Civil War Stanton concentrated her efforts on abolishing slavery, and she became more outspoken. In 1868 she and Anthony worked on The Revolution, a militant weekly paper.

Elizabeth Blackwell (1821-1910) was a British physician and the first woman to receive a medical degree in the United States. In the mid 1857 she opened a clinic that became known as the New York Infirmary for Poor Women and Children, an institution that would last for more than a century. She created a medical school for women in the late 1860's.[3]

Lucy Stone (1819-1893) Born in Massachusetts, Lucy Stone dedicated her life to improving the rights of American women. She supported the Women's National Loyal League and in 1866 helped found the American Equal Rights Association. She also organized and was elected the president of the State Woman's Suffrage Association of New Jersey and spent her life serving the cause. She died 30 years before women were finally permitted to vote. [4]

Victoria Woodhull (1838-1927) was a spiritualist, activist, politician and author who was the first woman to run for the presidency of the United States. She was a free thinker who created "Woodhull and Claflin's Weekly" a radical publication, in 1870, with her sister, Tennessee. It gave the sisters a place to express their ideas on social reforms, including women's suffrage, birth control and free love. She became a target for public scrutiny because of her many relationships and radical ideas. [5]

Jane Addams (1860-1935) co-founded one of the first settlements in the U.S., the Hull House (provided services for the immigrant and poor population living in the Chicago area), in Chicago in 1889, and was named a co-winner of the 1931 Nobel Peace Prize. She also served as the first female president of the National Conference of Social work, established the National Federation of Settlements and served as president of the Women's International League for Peace and Freedom. [6]

Alice Paul (1885-1977) dedicated her life's work to women's rights and was a key figure in the push for the 19th Amendment. She was born in New Jersey, studied at Swarthmore College in 1905 and went on to do graduate work in New York City and England. While in London from 1906 to 1909, Paul became politically active and unafraid to use dramatic tactics in support of a cause. She joined the women's suffrage movement in Britain and was arrested on several occasions, serving time in jail and going on a hunger strike. She returned to the States in 1910 and became involved in the women's suffrage movement there as well. Driven also to change other laws that affected women, she earned a Ph.D. from the University of Pennsylvania in 1912.

Paul organized parades and pickets in support of suffrage. Her first- and the largest was in Washington, DC on March 3, 1913, the day before President-elect Woodrow Wilson's inauguration. Approximately 8,000 women marched with banners and floats down Pennsylvania Avenue from the Capitol to the White House, while a half million spectators watched, supported and harassed the marchers. On the 17th they met with Wilson who said it was not yet time for an amendment to the Constitution. In January 1917, Paul and over 1,000 "Silent Sentinels" began eighteen months of picketing the White House, standing at the gates with such signs as, "Mr. President, how long must women wait for liberty?" They endured verbal and physical attacks from spectators, which increased after the US entered World War I. Instead of protecting the women's right to free speech and peaceful assembly, the police arrested them on the flimsy charge of obstructing traffic. Paul was sentenced to jail for seven months, where she organized a hunger strike in protest. Doctors threatened to send Paul to an insane asylum and force-fed her, while newspaper accounts of her treatment garnered public sympathy and support for suffrage. It took two more years for the Senate, House, and the required 36 states to approve the amendment. [7]

Maud Wood Park (1871-1955)
Maud Wood Park not only aided female voters as the first president of the League of Women Voters, but she

also helped form and chaired the Women's Joint Congressional Committee, which lobbied Congress to enact legislation favored by women's groups. One law that Park and the committee pushed for was the Sheppard-Towner Maternity Bill (1921). In 1918, the United States, when compared to other industrialized countries, had ranked a disheartening 17th in maternal death; this bill provided money to take care of women during and after pregnancy — at least until its funding was ended in 1929.

Park also lobbied for the Cable Act (1922), which let most American women who married foreign nationals keep their citizenship. The legislation was far from perfect — it had a racist exception for people of Asian descent — but it at least recognized that married women had identities separate from their husbands. [8]

Mary McLeod Bethune (1875-1955) For African American women, getting the vote often didn't mean being able to cast a ballot. But Mary McLeod Bethune, a well-known activist and educator, was determined that she and other women would exercise their rights. Bethune raised money to pay the poll tax in Daytona, Florida (she got enough for 100 voters), and also taught women how to pass their literacy tests. Even facing off with the Ku Klux Klan couldn't keep Bethune from voting.

Bethune's activities didn't stop there; she founded the National Council of Negro Women in 1935 to advocate for Black women. And during the presidency of Franklin D. Roosevelt, she accepted a position as director for the Division of Negro Affairs in the National Youth Administration. This made her the highest-ranking African American woman in government. Bethune knew she was setting an example, stating, "I visualized dozens of Negro women coming after me, filling positions of high trust and strategic importance."[9]

Rose Schneiderman (1909-1964) A former factory worker and dedicated labor organizer, Rose Schneiderman focused on the needs of working women post-suffrage. She did this while holding various positions: From 1926 to 1950, Schneiderman was president of the Women's Trade Union League; she was the only woman on the National Recovery Administration's Labor Advisory Board; and she served as New York State's Secretary of Labor from 1937 to 1943.

During the Great Depression, Schneiderman called for unemployed female workers to get relief funds. She wanted domestic workers (who were almost all women) to be covered by Social Security, a change that took place 15 years after the law was first enacted in 1935. Schneiderman also sought to improve wages and working conditions for waitresses, laundry workers, beauty parlor workers and hotel maids, many of whom were women of color. [10]

Eleanor Roosevelt (1884-1962) The wife of President Franklin D. Roosevelt, Eleanor changed the role of the first lady through her participation in American politics. Not content to stay in the background, she gave press conferences and spoke out for human rights, children's causes and women's issues, working on behalf of the League of Women Voters. She penned her own newspaper column, "My Day," and focused on helping the country's poor, stood against racial discrimination and during World War II, traveled abroad to visit US troops. President Harry Truman appointed Eleanor as a delegate to the United Nations General Assembly and she chaired the committee which drafted The Universal Declaration of Human Rights, an effort that she considered to be her greatest achievement. President John F. Kennedy reappointed her to the United States delegation to the U.N. in 1961, and later named her to the National Advisory Committee of the Peace Corps and as chair of the President's Commission on the Status of Women [11]

Margaret Sanger (1879-1966) felt that "no woman can call herself free who does not own and control her own body" – for her accessible birth control was a necessary part of women's rights. In the 1920's Sanger put aside earlier radical tactics in order to focus on getting mainstream support for legal contraception. She founded the American Birth Control League in 1921; two years later her Birth Control Clinical Research Bureau opened its doors. The Bureau kept detailed patient records that proved the efficacy and safety of birth control. Sanger also lobbied for birth control legislation, though she didn't meet with much success. However, she had more luck in court, with the U.S.

Court of Appeals ruling in 1936 that it was okay to import and distribute birth control for medical purposes. And Sanger's advocacy also helped shift public attitudes: The Sears catalog ended up selling "preventives" and in a *1938 Ladies Home Journal* poll, 79% of its readers supported legal birth control. [12]

African American Women and the Nineteenth Amendment

African American women, though often overlooked in the history of woman suffrage, engaged in significant reform efforts and political activism leading to and following the ratification in 1920 of the Nineteenth Amendment, which barred states from denying American women the right to vote on the basis of their sex. They had as much – or more – at stake in the struggle as white women. From the earliest years of the suffrage movement, Black women worked side by side with white suffragists. By the late nineteenth century, however, as the suffrage movement splintered off the issue of race in the years after the Civil War, Black women formed their own organizations to continue their efforts to secure and protect the rights of all women, and men.

The US women's rights movement was closely allied with the antislavery movement, and before the Civil War Black and white abolitionists and suffragists joined together in common cause. During the antebellum period, a small cohort of formerly enslaved and free Black women, including **Sojourner Truth (1797-1883)**, **Harriet Tubman (1820-1913), Maria W. Stewart (1803-1879), Henrietta Purvis (1833-1925) , Harriet Forten Purvis (1810-1875), (Sarah Remond (1826-1894), and Mary Ann Shadd Cary (1823-1893),** were active in women's rights circles. They were joined in their advocacy of the women's rights and suffrage by prominent Black men, including **Frederick Douglass, Charles Lenox, Remond and Robert Purvis,** and worked in collaboration with white abolitionists and women's rights activists, including **William Lloyd Garrison, Elizabeth Cady Stanton and Susan B. Anthony.**

Following the 1848 women's rights convention in Seneca Falls, New York, prominent free Black women abolitionists and suffragists attended, spoke and assumed leadership positions at multiple women's rights gatherings through the 1850's and 1860's. In 1851, former slave **Sojourner Truth** delivered her famous "Aint I a Woman" speech at the National Women's Rights Convention in Akron, Ohio. **Sara Remond** and her brother Charles won wide acclaim for their pro-woman suffrage speeches at the 1858 National Women's Rights Convention in New York City.

With the end of the Civil War, arguments for woman suffrage became entwined with debates over the rights of former slaves and the meaning of citizenship. Sisters **Margaretta For**ten and **Harriet Forten Purvis**, who helped to establish the interracial Philadelphia

Suffrage Association in 1866, and other Black women were active in the new American Equal Rights Association (AERA), an organization formed by former abolitionists and women's rights advocates that endorsed both women's and Black men's right to vote. Purvis served on the AERA executive committee. Abolitionist **Frances Ellen Watkins Harper** (1825-1911) spoke on behalf of woman suffrage at the founding meeting of the AERA, and **Sojourner Truth** gave a major address at its first anniversary meeting.

But with the proposal of the Fifteenth Amendment, which would enfranchise Black men but not women, interracial and mixed-gender coalitions began to deteriorate. Suffragists had to choose between insisting on universal rights or accepting the priority of Black male suffrage. The split in the suffrage movement over the Fifteenth Amendment prompted **Elizabeth Cady Stanton and Susan B. Anthony** to sever ties with the AERA and form the National Woman Suffrage Association (NWSA), which promoted universal suffrage, insisting that Black men should not receive the vote before white women. Stanton and Anthony's racist remarks about Black men evoked intense anger on the part of Black suffragists, including long-time allies **Frederick Douglass** and **Frances Ellen Watkins Harper**. As a result, Harper supported the Fifteenth Amendment—this from a fiercely independent woman who believed women were equal, indeed, superior to men in their level of productivity; men were talkers, while women were doers. Harper joined the new American Woman Suffrage Association (AWSA), which supported both Black suffrage and woman suffrage and took a state-by-state approach to securing women's right to vote. As Harper proclaimed in her closing remarks at the 1873 AWSA convention, "much as white women need the ballot, colored women need it more."[1] As many whites, including some white female suffragists, publicly denounced Black male suffrage, Black women incorporated Black male suffrage as an important component of their suffrage goals.

Black women, however, did become members of both woman suffrage groups—the **Stanton** and **Anthony**–led NWSA and the **Lucy Stone** and **Julia Ward Howe**–led AWSA. **Hattie Purvis** was a delegate to the NWSA (as well as a member of the executive committee of the Pennsylvania State Suffrage Association). Among the prominent African American reformers and suffragists who joined the AWSA were **Charlotte Forten (1837-1914) and Josephine St. Pierre Ruffin (1842-1924),** a member of the Massachusetts Woman Suffrage Association.

Black women attended and spoke out at political and religious meetings and public rallies. Their enthusiasm and political engagement within and outside suffrage campaigns was particularly concerning to whites in the post-emancipation South.[1] The suffrage work of **Charlotte ("Lottie") Rollin (1849-?)** shows the long history of African American women's political activism outside the Northeast and beyond women's rights conferences and organizations. In 1866, a year before chairing the inaugural meeting of the South

Carolina Woman's Rights Association, Rollin courageously proclaimed her support for universal suffrage at a meeting of the South Carolina House of Representatives. In 1870, she was the elected secretary of the South Carolina Woman's Rights Association, an affiliate of the AWSA. Rollin, along with her sisters Frances and Louisa and other local women, figured prominently in Reconstruction politics and woman suffrage campaigns at the local and national levels in the early 1870s. South Carolina's African American woman suffrage advocates were encouraged by African American men. In certain 1870 South Carolina district elections, Black election officials encouraged attempted to vote Black women to vote—an action the Rollins sisters and some other African American women were already assuming (or attempting) on their own. In 1871, pioneer suffragist, newspaper editor, and first female law school student at Howard University **Mary Ann Shadd Cary**, with several other women, attempted, unsuccessfully, to register to vote in Washington, DC. This failure notwithstanding, they insisted upon and secured an official signed affidavit recognizing that they had.

Like white suffragists, African American women linked suffrage to a multitude of political and economic issues in order to further their cause and engaged in multiple strategies to secure women's political and voting rights within and outside the organized suffrage movement. At the same time, they combated anti-Black discrimination in the southern United States and within the predominantly white national woman suffrage

23

organizations.

Over time, tensions between Stanton, Anthony, and Douglass subsided. The discrimination against Black women in the woman suffrage movement continued as certain white woman suffragist leaders sought southern white male and female support. The anti-Black rhetoric and actions of NWSA leaders Susan B. Anthony and Elizabeth Cady Stanton persisted but so did African American women's courageous battles for both gender and racial equality. In 1876, Cary wrote to leaders of the National Woman Suffrage Association urging them to place the names of ninety-four Washington, DC, woman suffragists on their Declaration of the Rights of the Women of the United States issued on the one-hundredth anniversary of American Independence, which concluded, "we ask justice, we ask equality, we ask that all the civil and political rights that belong to citizens of the United States, be guaranteed to us and our daughters forever." While unsuccessful in having their names added, Cary remained a committed suffrage activist, speaking at the 1878 NWSA meeting. Two years later, she formed the Colored Woman's Franchise Association in Washington, DC, which linked suffrage not just to political rights but to education and labor issues.

Fannie Lou Hamer was a women's rights activist, voting rights activist, and community organizer. She was raised in rural Mississippi where she and her family worked as sharecroppers. In her quest to register to vote, she lost her job, endured countless threats, and was brutalized at the orders of the police while in custody at the Winona county jail.

Once she was finally registered and able to vote, Hamer founded, along with other organizers, the Mississippi Freedom Democratic Party (MFDP) to register African Americans to vote and challenge the all-white Democratic delegation from Mississippi. In 1964, she ran for Congress and, along with the MFDP, traveled to Atlantic City to demand a Mississippi delegate seat at the Democratic National Convention. Against the wishes of President Lyndon Johnson, Hamer testified before the convention's Credentials Committee, capturing national attention. During her testimony, Hamer detailed the brutal attack she endured in Winona jail, along with other barriers Black folks in the South were facing in order to vote. Her speech encouraged other Black folks to register to vote and brought much needed attention to the disenfranchisement that was taking place in the South.

Thanks to the efforts of Fannie Lou Hamer, the Mississippi Freedom Democratic Party, and countless others who raised the importance of voting rights for all—not just a privileged few, Lyndon B Johnson signed the Voting Rights Act (VRA) into law the following year. The VRA declared that no person should be denied the right to vote on account of color or race and outlawed discriminatory registration practices such as literacy test, which led to 250,000 Black folks registering to vote by the end of 1965. [13]

There is so much more to read about these amazing women. Go to: https://www.nps.gov/articles/african-american-women-and-the-nineteenth-amendment.htm and see more about women like Rosa Parks, Sojourner Truth, Ida B. Wells, Ella Baker, Septima Clark, Fannie Lou Hamer, Audre Lourde, Marsha P. Johnson, Alicia Garza, Patrisse Khan-Cullors, Harriet Tubman, Dorothy Height and Opal Tometi.

Women of the 20th & 21st Century

Women continued the fight for their rights in the mid 1900's and beyond. A few of these important women were:

Gloria Steinem   Aptly referred to as the "Mother of Feminism, Gloria Steinem led the women's liberation movements throughout the '60's and '70's – and continues to do so today.   She is a writer, political activist, and feminist organizer. She was a founder of *New York* and *Ms.* magazines, and i*s the author of The Truth Will Set You Free, But First It Will Piss You Off, My Life on the Road, Moving Beyond Words, Revolution from Within,* and *Outrageous Acts and Everyday Rebellions,* all published in the United States, and in India, *As If Women Matter.* She co-founded the National Women's Political Caucus, the Ms. Foundation for Women, the Free to Be Foundation, and the Women's Media Center in the United States. As links to other countries, she helped found Equality Now, Donor Direct Action, and Direct Impact Africa. For her writing, Steinem has

26

received the Penney-Missouri Journalism Award, the Front Page and Clarion awards, the National Magazine Award, the Lifetime Achievement in Journalism Award from the Society of Professional Journalists, the Society of Writers Award from the United Nations, and the University of Missouri School of Journalism Award for Distinguished Service in Journalism. In 1993, her concern with child abuse led her to co-produce an Emmy Award–winning TV documentary for HBO, *Multiple Personalities: The Search for Deadly Memories.* She and Amy Richards co-produced a series of eight documentaries on violence against women around the world for VICELAND in 2016. In 2013, she was awarded the Presidential Medal of Freedom by President Barack Obama. In 2019, she received the Freedom Award from the National Civil Rights Museum. She is the subject of Julie Taymor's upcoming biopic, *The Glorias,* set to premier in Fall 2020.[14]

Betty Friedan Betty Friedan was an American feminist, writer and activist. A leading figure in the women's movement in the United States, her 1963 book The Feminine Mystique is often credited with sparking the second wave of American feminism in the 20th century. In 1966, Friedan co-founded and was elected the first president of the National Organization for Women (NOW), which aimed to bring women "into the mainstream of American society now [in] fully equal partnership with men". In 1970, after stepping down as NOW's first president, Friedan organized the nationwide Women's Strike for Equality on August 26, the 50th anniversary of the Nineteenth Amendment to the United States Constitution granting women the right to vote. The national strike was successful in broadening the feminist movement; the march led by Friedan in New York City alone attracted over 50,000 people. In 1971, Friedan joined other leading feminists to establish the National Women's Political Caucus. Friedan was also a strong supporter of the proposed Equal Rights Amendment to the United States Constitution that passed the United States House of Representatives (by a vote of 354–24) and Senate (84–8) following intense pressure by women's groups led by NOW in the early 1970s. Following Congressional passage of the amendment, Friedan advocated for ratification of the amendment in the states and supported other women's rights reforms; she founded the National Association for the Repeal of Abortion Laws but was later critical of the abortion-centered positions of many liberal feminists.

Regarded as an influential author and intellectual in the United States, Friedan remained active in politics and advocacy until the late 1990s, authoring six books. As early as the 1960s Friedan was critical of polarized and extreme factions of feminism that attacked groups such as men and homemakers. One of her later books, *The Second Stage* (1981), critiqued what Friedan saw as the extremist excesses of some feminists.[15]

Angela Yvonne Davis (born 1944) is an American political activist, philosopher, academic, and author. She is a professor emerita at the University of California, Santa Cruz. Ideologically a Marxist, Davis was a longtime member of the Communist Party USA (CPUSA) and is a founding member of the Committees of Correspondence for Democracy and Socialism (CCDS). She is the author of over ten books on class, feminism, race, and the US prison system. [16]

Hillary Diane Rodham Clinton (née Rodham; born October 26, 1947) is an American politician, diplomat, lawyer, writer, and public speaker who served as the 67th United States secretary of state from 2009 to 2013, as a United States senator from New York from 2001 to 2009, and as First Lady of the United States from 1993 to 2001. Clinton became the first woman to be nominated for president of the United States by a major political party when she won the Democratic Party nomination in 2016. She was the first woman to win the popular vote in an American presidential election, which she lost to Donald Trump.[17]

Ruth Bader Ginsburg became the second female justice of the U.S. Supreme Court. Born in 1933 in Brooklyn, New York, Bader taught at Rutgers University Law School and then at Columbia University, where she became its first female tenured professor. She served as the director of the Women's Rights Project of the American Civil Liberties Union during the 1970s, and was appointed to the U.S. Court of Appeals for the District of Columbia in 1980. Named to the U.S. Supreme Court in 1993 by President Bill Clinton, she continued to argue for gender equality in such cases as United States v. Virginia. She died

September 18, 2020 due to complications from metastatic pancreas cancer at the age of 87.

In her earlier years Ginsburg transferred to Columbia Law School in New York City to join her husband, where she was elected to the school's law review. She graduated first in her class in 1959. Despite her outstanding academic record, however, Ginsburg continued to encounter gender discrimination while seeking employment after graduation. After clerking for U.S. District Judge Edmund L. Palmieri, she taught at Rutgers University Law School (1963-72) and at Columbia (1972-80), where she became the school's first female tenured professor.[18]

Kamala Harris (born October 20, 1964, Oakland, California, U.S.), 49th vice president of the United States (2021) in the Democratic administration of President Joe Biden. She was the first woman and the first African American to hold the post being inaugurated on January 20th, 2021. Her father was Jamaican and her mother was from India. She had previously served in the U.S. Senate (2017–21) and as the first Indian American in the Senate and just the second Black woman. She served as attorney general of California (2011–17). She worked at deputy district attorney in Oakland, CA (1990-1998), district attorney in 2004 and was elected as attorney general in 2010. She was elected to the US Senate in 2015 and Joe Biden chose her as his running mate in 2020. [19]

One of the women we owe a debt to that you might not know about, who made great accomplishments and was not recognized as men were, and who made similar strides is **Cecilia Payne**.

Since her death in 1979, the woman who discovered what the universe is made of has not so much as received a memorial plaque. Her newspaper obituaries do not mention her greatest discovery. Every high school student knows that Isaac Newton discovered gravity, that Charles Darwin discovered evolution, and that Albert Einstein discovered the relativity of time. But when it comes to the composition of our universe, the textbooks simply say that the most abundant atom in the universe is hydrogen. And no one ever wonders how we know." — Jeremy Knowles, discussing the complete lack of recognition Cecilia Payne gets, even today, for her revolutionary discovery. (via alliterate)

OH WAIT, LET ME TELL YOU ABOUT CECILIA PAYNE

• Cecilia Payne won a scholarship to Cambridge.

• Cecilia Payne completed her studies, but Cambridge wouldn't give her a degree because she was a woman, so she said to heck with that and moved to the United States to work at Harvard.

• Cecilia Payne was the first person ever to earn a Ph.D. in astronomy from Radcliffe College, with what Otto Strauve called "the most brilliant Ph.D. thesis ever written in astronomy."

• Not only did Cecilia Payne discover what the universe is made of, she also discovered what the sun is made of (Henry Norris Russell, a fellow astronomer, is usually given credit for discovering that the sun's composition is different from the Earth's, but he came to his conclusions four years later than Payne — after telling her not to publish).

• Cecilia Payne is the reason we know basically anything about variable stars (stars whose brightness as seen from earth fluctuates). Literally every other study on variable stars is based on her work.

• Cecilia Payne was the first woman to be promoted to full professor from within Harvard and the first woman to head a science department at Harvard. She also inspired entire generations of women to take up science.

• Cecilia Payne is awesome and everyone should know her. [20]

A few other women who were first in their field or made great strides for women: Madeleine Albright, Bella Abzug, Malala Yousafzai, Coretta Scott King, Lady Bird Johnson, Alice Paul, Dorothy Day, Lucy Burns, Margaret Mead, Geraldine A. Ferraro, Mary Mahoney and the list goes on. There are so many more and a wealth of information awaits you on the internet about these great women activists. [21]

The following are many of the comments, positive and negative, from women and men, young and old regarding women's rights. You are pretty much sure to find some with which you agree! Comments are printed as they were received without corrections.

Comments: Printed as received without editing.

"I wasn't born in 1940, I grew up in this mess. My father was not a nice father, my first husband informed me that me & our kids were his "chattel." I was beaten, raped and strangled & could get no help, nor birth control. I was in fear of my & my kids lives & we ran away. It was tough going, but after 3 years I bought us a house, then he found us! Still no help from the authorities, we were still on our own! Now the government wants us to go back to that? NOT ON YOUR LIFE!" **(Jane Martin)**

"Thank you for the summary. In 1970 I founded the Name Choice Center for CA Women. Women don't realize that we had no choice unless we did not marry to use our husband's name. He owned us even as late as the 70's. We could not have a credit card without using his name, or own property. In other words we were Mrs. Him. Our history was absorbed into his family and most women took it for granted. I researched the issue, traveled the State to inform people they had a choice without going to court. Our law is based on English Common law." **(Pat Montandon)**

"A beautiful reminder of women's history that is not always known as a truth. Beautiful....I'm in tears!" **(Nell Powers Gwinn)**

"The effort to remove rights from women continues with the "Fathers For Equal Rights" movement which is anything but equal, but rather for removing a woman's basic right to raise her own children. Abused women and children face insurmountable obstacles in courts and gender bias so prevalent that law schools have classes on the subject. FFR supplies men with legal

33

assistance for little or no money, while women who qualify for "legal aid" are turned away 80% of the time. FFR is a powerful group of men with mass funding lobbying Washington and encouraging men to abuse their children to make the mothers appear unstable and are driven by their desire to escape the responsibility of child support. This movement was unfortunately supported by our government when Richard Nixon passed The Fatherhood Initiative to give men an advantage in custody cases so government funding would not be necessary to enforce child support in a society where divorce had become socially acceptable. Women were considered more compliant and therefore more likely to financially support their children that were ripped out of their care. Every aspect of American culture remains controlled by men for men including government, business, law, religion and education. YouTube has an outdated but eye-opening video composed by lawyers on the removal of women's legal rights called, "Small Justice: Little Justice in American Courts." Every abused woman needs to know as the gap widens." **(Betty Hobbs Krenik)**

"My mother was 31 when my father died in 1945, leaving my mom with 4 small children. She had a credit card and sold the house we lived in and bought another in 1954. As far as I know she never had a problem with credit, etc." **(Charlotte Melching-Croteau)**

"I am stunned by this information. Thank you for presenting this interesting and honest history. Women are amazing and deserve credit for the fight. I am proud to be a woman and so deeply proud of the great, brave

34

women who blazed this trail with energy and strength. Thank you. We must continue to fight and we will. Never underestimate the power of a woman." **(Sylvia Gittleman)** Lebanon Valley College Alumni

"Thank you for gracious recall of a difficult past in American civil society. I remember being with a group of young women who were shocked in disbelief that in the 60's they could not open a checking account on their own without a man's approval." ("**Sahar Taman**) University of Chicago

"This is an awesome article. I believe in human rights and I believe that women's rights are included in there as well. Every faction seems to have good intentions, at first, and after a time their usefulness isn't as pressing. Then, in trying to justify its existence, eccentricities and malice begins to infect the good intentions. A prime example is labor unions. A university student could write a thesis on that one. I heard tell that if you want to fight a monster, be careful lest you become one yourself." **(G. Gideon** Wells)

1875 **Minor v Happersett, 88 U.S. 162 (1875): The U.S. Supreme Court declares that despite the privileges and immunities clause, a state can prohibit a woman from voting. The court declares women as "persons," but holds that they constitute a special category of nonvoting citizens."**
1900 **By now, every state has passed legislation modeled after New York's Married Women's**

Property Act (1848) granting married women some control over their property and earnings.
(note that it says "some control".)

"Remember the whole part of this little story of our lives as women. The equal rights amendment DID NOT PASS so our rights can be revoked by the President's stroke of a pen. Don't you lose sight of that Fact. A library card fails very short on my list for demands of equal rights. Women are feeling unsafe with reason as our basic rights are being discussed and decided by the same kind of men to took them away in the first place. I think it is beyond time for an Amendment that guarantees it" (**Judy Salerna**)

"Thank you for such a concise article. I hope it will be read by many."(**Christine Courtley**) University of Massachusetts Amhurst

"As a man I am ashamed. Eye Opener." (**Jim JD Ditton**)

"In 1966 when I got married my name was Louise Belec, turned into Albert Lavigne and I had to call myself Albert. I couldn't use the name Louise, only Mrs Albert Lavigne." (**Nicole Tmj Lavigne Stoker**)

"Thank you for abstract, enjoyed and trust your comments. I am a Lakota grandma/unci who will tag all my grand children for this article." Pilamayeksto (**Kay Keyoka**)

"I got married in 1964. In 1965 we decided to buy life insurance. I had made the decision to keep my birth surname. When I signed the insurance document with that name the agent was furious with me and tore up the document. He told my husband to educate me a little and he would come back with new documents for my proper signature.(Mrs. Jane Doe) I told him not to bother." **(Sharon Anne Matheson)**

"My great grandmother inherited money which she was not allowed to have. It went to her husband. In 1919 my grandmother went to jail for insisting she be allowed to vote. In 1973 my mother, a nurse, was paid $2 an hour less than the first male nurse hired by the hospital. I am fortunate to have these stories. They keep me fighting." **(Anne Eckhart)**

1920 The Nineteenth Amendment to the U.S. Constitution is ratified. It declares: "The right of citizens of the United States to vote shall not be denied or abridged by the United States or by any State on account of sex.
<u>100 years ago August 2020!!</u>

"Thank you for this message to us. I remember a time when we could work for very low wages, put people through college and still not be able to enter into contracts or have credit on our own. Yes, many brave women have battle for us and it is encouraging to see enlightened men standing beside us now." **(Connie Schied)**

"Women could, and did, own property in the 19th century. Nashville's own Adelicia Acklen had her 2nd husband sign a prenuptial agreement. Also, women homesteaders were fairly common." **(Kim Feathers Caudell)** Hollywood High School.

S Weeks Response: "Fascinating article. You might enjoy reading "Proud Spirit" about Helga Esby, but the laws I was referring to applied to married women in urban areas and not to homesteaders who had to be amazing women!"

KFC replied: "You did not specify, you just said "women," which implies all women."

S Weeks Response: "She is correct and I responded to that."

"We must never take for granted what so many of our sisters fought and sacrificed for. We owe them to at least recognize and honor their sacrifices by being active participants to bring about a more equal and just system for all women worldwide. It's not just about you and your life, it encompasses all women worldwide!" **(Dodie Horgan)** Pittsburg State University

"This is some great history of the women's movement from years past. In Iran a woman still can't own property and if their husbands die, they and their children hit the streets, literally. I believe woman have the upper hand on the white male today." **(Jamie Arnold)** Richland High School

"When my father died in 1986 my mother was told she had no credit! She had no checking account! She was the added name on my father's checking account and credit cards. She was not allowed to get a credit card in her own name then!! She lived in a paid-for million dollar house, had 2 masters degrees and multiple philanthropic jobs. She set up and ran Project Transition in Detroit for women coming out of prison with no job skills. She started the Christ Child Society group in Florida when they moved there! She was so frustrated! Things are so different now! Let's hope we do not regress in time." (**Chery Simons McGee**) Seattle, WA

"In the 1980's here in Nevada when my parents started divorce proceedings, my mother's credit cards – from 30 years BEFORE she had been married – were cancelled by my father's attorney without her knowledge. The companies just assumed that "the husband" had rights which superseded his wife's. Later, the judge in our community property state determined that all community assets would be split 80-20 since my father had the higher earnings despite the fact that most of the wealth came from her family through inheritance. She fought unsuccessfully because – no matter WHAT newer laws say – old attitudes take decades to change, and men still retain most of the power to interpret the laws." (**Ann Ward Cummings**) Las Vegas, Nevada

"A lot of this is true, but are you saying it's ok for people to break our laws to come here and get free insurance, welfare, food stamps, while we have children starving, vet living on the streets, people who can't afford Obamacare getting fined, people looking for work while illegals are here getting jobs and sending the money back to Mexico? Complaining about a barrier between US and Mexico saying it's evil yet they have no problem with Mexico building a border between them and other South American countries to keep them out. And finally what does dressing up like Purple haired vagina supposed to.." **(Leonard van Duyn)** Dog Trainer

"I applied for a credit card and they requested my husband's income on the application form. I was offended and stated that my income and credit rating could support the credit card just fine. They refused without his information. I replied with my marital status being single and I received the credit card. The fact that if you are married, you still require your husband's information is barbaraic, especially if your income is higher than his. This was maybe 15 years ago, and I thought things had changed, until last year I applied for a business line of credit for MY business. Exact same company. I changed to single and I received the line of credit. So there's still work to be done here." **(Louise Lynch Rose)**

"Here in Canada I had to fight tooth and nail to get my own credit rating in 1976." **(Ann Power)** St. John's, Newfoundland and Labrador

> **1937 The U.S. Supreme Court upholds Washington State's minimum wage laws for women.**

> **1938 The Fair Labor Standards Act establishes minimum wage without regard to sex.**

"Complacency landed Trump the election, he won only 23% of the votes, because of the 40% who didn't vote. It's a dark time in our history. Let's not let it rewrite the past fifty years of gains. Women's rights are human rights!" **(Linda S. Morre)** Saint Mary's College of California

"1973 Roe v Wade. We won't go back!" **(Karen Reilly)** Medina, Ohio

"Those who don't know history are doomed to repeat it. Fight for your rights." **(BJ Doty)** Scripps College

"I would add the importance of technology. The bicycle enabled women to travel out on their own. The typewriter got women into the office. Improved technology has decreased the value of muscle and increased the value of brain power. Information technology has enabled everyone to be providers of information, not just men." **(Paul J Chamberlain)**

"Thank you. I believe as recently as the 1970's women had a hard time getting credit on their own." **(Linda Bryant Halvorson)** Chippewa Falls, WI

"ALL RIGHTS ARE REVOKABLE, AND QUICKLY. JUST ASK THE CITIZENS OF TURKEY, TODAY ASK THEM HOW DIFFERENT THEIR COUNTRY IS THIS YEAR FROM WHAT IS WAS LAST YEAR." **(Jeannette B**lankenship) California Polytechnic State University

"Most of my friends are loving, caring, say yes to equal rights, people you would want as good friends. They are also women." **(Mark Richards)**

"Thank you Sharon Weeks! An excellent summary of some of the highlights in women's history in the U.S. We need more reminders of just how often women are not treated equally by those in power. It is amazing that in an era when women are better educated, own more businesses, and, on average, outlive men – that women don't hold more and higher positions in our government." **(Ed Kowlieski)** Madison, Wisconsin

> **1961 In Hoyt v. Florida, 368 U.S. 57 (1961): The U. S. Supreme Court upholds rules adopted by the State of Florida that made it far less likely for women than men to be called for jury service on the grounds that a "woman is still regarded as the center of home and family life."**

"**Lucy Baines Johnson**, daughter of President Lyndon Johnson, was denied admission to Georgetown University. She had recently been married and was told she needed to pursue her career in the home, Not college." **(Corey Jones)**

S Weeks Response: "In 1965 she was asked to choose between marriage and college. After two semesters she chose marriage. Fifty-two years after she dropped out she was invited back to campus to serve as a commencement speaker for Georgetown's School of Nursing and Health Studies, at age 70, and was awarded an honorary doctorate."

"Lest we forget." **(Ken Kidder)** Woodstock, Georgia

"I am not that old, but as a retired school teacher and administrator, I can tell you that when I entered the teaching profession in 1979, the sexual harassment I endured in the teacher's lounge by many of the male teachers drove me to eating in the cafeteria with the middle school students. I was never taken seriously by my then principal. I worked twice as hard to prove myself as the men did in the school and I did not make the same rate of pay as they did for their lazy ethic. We have to keep fighting so things get better and do not go back to the way they were." **(Carol Sorvig)** Adjunct Faculty & U Supervisor at U of Redlands School of Education

"Never give up fight for what is right, women will always be the stronger sex and unlimited amount of patience our weapon." **(Susanne Apostolakos)** Chestermere, Alberta

"Basically I lost my reply saying that the young women need more momentum to back the passing of ERA! We fought hard to get it passed but the male lawmakers thought it would be better to pass legislation piecemeal or individual laws instead of giving us the whole enchalotta (one amendment) that covers everything we need. We have laws like maternity leave which varies by State. An ERA amendment would make the law the same for each State!!! I thank you, Sharon Weeks, for your history. I am a past member of the International Women's Year Committee (IWY) of the State of Connecticut and mandated by The USA State Dept. who invited me to serve with other women by the Carter Administration. There is a lot of history to IWY which held meetings in most USA states on women's issues and fed into the meetings in Houston TX and Niarobi Kenya. I hope that we as feminists will continue to make strides forward." **(Judy Guy)** University of New Haven

"Thank you! I totally agree with you!! We should be expressing gratitude rather than demands!!! We have more freedom to a blessed life than any country in the world!!! God Bless American!! Praise God!!!" **(Sandra Plunk Haddock)** Realtor, Coldwell Banker Apex

"I wish my nieces would read this. They would roll their eyes and get impatient with me whenever I would make a feminist comment (and tell me that feminism wasn't needed any more." **(Stephanie Skemp)** North Canton, Ohio

"So well said" **(Shelia Horton)** Simon Fraser University, B.C., Canada

"A very timely post! And as a man I wholly support and defend the rise and wisdom and rights of my sisters." (**Gary R. Markley**) Orthotist at Hanger C1

"It seems to me what women do NOT know is the threat of Radical Islam and Sharia Law trying to infiltrate into our court system. We live in the greatest country on earth and women ARE equal to men. Instead of putting out this old feminist CRAP why don't you INFORM young women about the TOTAL LACK of rights for women in Muslim countries." (**Nancy Sinkule**) Freelancer

"I was 19 in 1966 when my new husband was sent off to boot camp during the Vietnam War. I could not get a bank account or lease an apartment. I had to live with his brother's family and later a room in my grandmother's house. I had a job but that made no difference. Young women could find themselves in a similar situation if our misogynistic president issues an executive order. We are not guaranteed equal rights under the constitution." (**Bonnie Griffin Kaake**) Co-Founder/Owner Plant-Based Lifestyle

"I believe Ms. Weeks has already lost it all. Her brains seem to have been eaten by the Liberal disease that leaves one deficient in logical thought." (**Steven Buending**) Toledo University
S Weeks: "I was so glad to get this comment, it had me laughing for days!"

"I remember when Oregon passed the ERA amendment. The challenge even back then was to explain to our legislators that just because "you treated your wife equally" did not mean that every woman had that constitutional right. Thank you for the recap! I am still very proud to say I have my Oregon "Women's Sewing Circle and Terrorist Society" 1977 T-shirt." (**Marta Hammel**) Retail Store Manager at Hughes Water Gardens

"Stand up ladies...I overheard a conversation just last week among a group of retired professional men supporting the Russian's government's reduction of spousal abuse to a misdemeanor. They openly support and we're commenting that we should apply that same standard here. I am so ashamed to admit there are some incredibly stupid gentlemen on my side of the gene pool. Your issues aren't women's issues, they are human issues. (**Scott Wojkowiak**)

"I am so grateful to you for summarizing the history of women's fight for rights. It is true that many young women don't know what it feels like to be treated like a piece of property. A woman may still have no control over her body and be forced to bear a genetically defective child after being raped by a father or brother. Women are still just a few years away from having no more rights than slaves. It is out of ignorance that women vote against their own interests. They idealize men or believe that only men can govern America. These women vote against abortion imagining their God is telling them to turn against their own safety and health care. Perhaps your message will get through to them." (**Gaynor Songer**) Student, Art Institute of Raleigh-Durham

"I part ways with the current Women's movement when it comes to the life of the unborn. With all due respect, I cannot understand how Women's Rights means pro-abortion, and how the direction changed. What I know of history, and from I've read, these great women suffergettes were against abortion, but were adamantly for equal rights. (**Renee Hanks**) Office Manager, Readding Stem Academy

"I wake up every day astounded that this topic and isolating and depravity targeted groups is still an argument. Despite the vast blanket of the "isms" now tolerated by congress and recognized by the President (I had a tough time capitalizing that) there are still universal and obvious rights and wrongs. I require neither religion or government to teach me the oobvious nor to attempt the obfuscation of the truth. I will not fight for someone I don't belive in. Our leaders may tell us that some of us are less valuable than others. I can tell them to go straight to Hell." (Feb. 7th, 2017) (**Ray Rogers**) Blacksmith at Medieval Ironworks Society

"Thank you for enlightening all of us. I was born in 1952 and have seen many changes for women's equality. You are right about today's young women. They probably think that it's always been this way. Let's get women's historical knowledge in history

47

books." **(Denise Williams)** Marion High School, Framingham, MA

"Thank you, will be having my teenage girls read this. Only thing you left out is referring to women as "bitches" which I assume refers to female dogs (viewed as property.) Disturbing trend among young women to refer to each other as "bitches" – wish they understood the implied meaning, and how hard women have had to fight for respect as well as legal rights." **(Meridith Pool Burnett)** Kennett Square, Pennsylvania

"Sucks." **(Tom Reed)** University of Texas at Austin

"A brilliantly written summary of an historical journey for the ladies in our country. They have persevered and to an extent prevailed, but the journey is not over." **(John Jackson)** Wharton School of the University of Pennsylvania

"Excellent summary and "alert." A few personal examples: 1959 – told I couldn't take HS chemistry as girls had no need for it. 1960 – told I couldn't take HS architectural drawing because girls could not be anything but nurses, secretaries or teachers. 1969-1970 was not allowed to continue to teach once my pregnancy showed." I was married. 1984- newly divorced and could not get gas or electric service restored to my home when my ex husband took it out of his name. Needed a males name on the account. Etc,. etc., etc. We are better off now, but there is still much to do!" (**Patti Rowe**) Grand Valley State University (retired)

"I recently watched the movie, "Suffragette." It showed me what happened to women who wanted to have rights. I cried seeing how many sacrificed their lives to fight for the freedoms we have. Many beaten by their husbands, many had their children taken away. The cruelty of man has no boundaries. I am 67 and I remember trying to leave an abusive husband. My name was on the deed of my house, but I had no credit to get an apartment. I felt so helpless. It's time, as women are experiencing such a level of disrespect from the President of the U.S. to formalize our equal rights with a Constitutional Amendment. It will not be given to us...we will have to fight for it." (**Judy Salerno**)

"It is so frustrating that the American attention span seems to be about two days long. When we function without a sense of history we are dangerously vulnerable to losing the rights and freedoms that others have sacrificed terribly to gain. We cannot afford to lose an inch of that hard won ground." (**Toddy Toney-grierson**) Retired

"Women have been fed these lies for so long we began to think we don't have it so bad and let it go thinking it will be okay. Eventually it comes up again. I got pregnant at 16. My parents gave me a choice to go to an orphanage and give the baby up for adoption or marry the guy and work it out. I married the guy; after I gave birth to two children and three year went by we divorced. I was too young to marry and too young to divorce. My parents signed. As years went by I read stories about some of the orphanages. Some of them had laundries where the young women worked to earn their keep. The prettier ones worked in offices, got fed well, but also endured rape and beatings. The laundry workers were fed very little, treated poorly. All lost their babies." **(Patricia Nolin)** University of Minnesota, Duluth

"A great History Lesson that every US Citizen should hear and we need to get rid of our current bigotted US President! Dump Trump ASAP!!" **(Stephen Obert)** Renton, Washington

"Go back even further in women's history and you'll see well over 2,000 years of purposeful oppression and subugation of women by women by men, dating back to Ancient Greece. Prior to then, there were Amazon women and matriarchal societies, but the men fought and beat the Amazon women. Thus began our long suffering under the strong arm of the patriarchy." **(Jeanne Berry)** Bowling Green, Ohio

"So many of society's inequalities are out in the open now, so if we let them go back into the shadows it will be on us...It's past time to step up to the plate." **(Wendy W. Williams)** Whittier College

"In 1961 I married and had a private scholarship to pay my tuition, but because I was pregnant, was refused admission into the Art Institute in Fort Wayne, Indiana. The director said I would be a bad influence on other students." **(Karen Moriarty)** Painting/Drawing Instructor at Artlink Contemporary Gallery

"Thanks for the reminders Sharon! Evermore work to do in achieving….Land of the Free, and the home of the Brave." **(Rob Barros)** Video System Engineer at NBA

"Thank you! We have a similar history in the UK and women in Switzerland did not get the vote till the 1960's. It's worth pointing out that while white women endured all this exclusion and violence, it was and is black women who bore the brunt of the institutionalized misogyny. And in huge areas of the world today, women and girls are still beaten, mutilated, sold and trafficked for their gender. Young women in priviledged parts of the world (the USA) perhaps have no idea how lucky they are and what struggles have gone on for them to be free. It did not happen by itself." **(Griselda Cann Murssett)** Distributor, Juice Plus+

"Lest we forget how far we have come, but how quickly it can go backwards! True story! More will be revealed, and we must not be deterred in this ongoing battle!" **(Michael Buchanan)** Purchasing Staff at Providence Kodiak Island Medical Center

"Timely, concise, and super important that men, women, and children know this history. It was fascinating to witness the process of one of my 6 year old granddaughters try to wrap her head around the fact that we've yet to EVER have a female President. We ran a woman to be President. That's our #1 reason....Trump won the Electoral College....we have work to do." Thank you. **(Rick Myers)**

"It is still not a crime to rape your wife in certain circumstances in some states. We have a long way to go." **(Charen Fegard)**

"Thank you for your summary. There continues to be mistreatment and injustice allowed against women in the U.S. Many see this as a problem in other countries alone, but if you're poor and without a support system, you are at risk. If you are not knowledgeable about your rights, you are at risk. If you're afraid to speak up for your rights, you are at risk. Women need to stand together and not pull each other apart. This is critically important in our current political environment. If you're a woman in a position of power, young or old, you should be speaking out so others more timid or fearful will join you. It is our responsibility now to help protect and enforce these hard won human rights." **(Lenore Jackson-Pope)** Boston Center for Memory

"I am 86 and have lived much of that or which you wrote. Thank you for reminding today's young women that they have battles yet ahead." **(Marilyn Alf)** Director of Clinical Social Work, Scripps Memorial Hospital, La Jolla, CA

"Girls, let's get off our comfortable butts and git'r done!" **(Jane Kreiswirth)** NY Botanical Garden, Retired Teacher

"Less we forget- the journey has been long, hard, and many times so demeaning. It is always a reminder how devastating "power over" can be. It exists today when we let any faction say "I am the way, and the only way," "I rule, you obey," "I own, and you never will if I can help it," and the list of "power over" tactics still continues and is a huge aphrodisiac to those who can capture and retain it- but always at the cost of so many others." (**Merry Maitre)**

"Awesome lady!!!" (**Paula Marsman**) Liceo de Ninas N°1 Santiago, Chili

"A very timely post! And as a man I wholly support, defend the rise and wisdom and rights of my sisters." (**Gary R. Markley)** Orthotist at Hanger Clinic

"A good read for the young women concerned with the color of their lipstick, but not the content of their minds." (**Eveline Horelle Daily**) Educated overseas by private tutors, Task master from the Sorbonne

"Fun article. Misleading in areas, but I understand you're trying to sway people's thoughts to your way of thinking....even if you leave some facts out and overstate others." (**Ray Roll)** **S Weeks Response**: "I think you misunderstood the purpose of the article. Telling women about women's suffrage in the early 1900's is not trying to sway, just to inform. If I omitted facts it was not intentional, newspapers don't allow you to go on for pages. Space restraints do limit how much one person can write. I really just want women to know where the rights they have today came from and that it is possible they (we) could lose them, to stay vigilant. Thanks for responding."

"Muslim women and their families ARE NOT being sent back to the terribly dangerous places they were trying so hard to flee" **(Tom McLaughlin)** Pius X High School, Lincoln, Nebraska **S Weeks Resp**onse: "We must read different newspapers, but thanks for responding."

"Wow. I never knew all those facts nor did I seek them out. It's amazing how far women have come and how far we still have to go to I be considered equal. Thank you for all your research and information, always BJ "**(Bon Joni Minotto-Collins)**

"The fight for a ratified ERA is very real and happening now!! Virginia, Nevada, and Illinois are poised to ratify. Virginia's Senate has ratified the federal ERA five times w/bipartisan support since 2011, only to get stuck in a very gerrymandered subcommittee in the House of Delegates. There are bills in Congress to move the Equal Rights Amendment forward and press the reset button. Call your Senators and Congress people from Hawaii to Maine and demand the co-patron SJRes5 (Speiers) and HJRes53 (Cardin) and take a stand for constitution equality once and for all. Only the Constitution conveys Constitutional right? Learn more at: Women-Matter.org#SimpleJusticeLongOverdue

#EqualMeansEqual "**(Eileen Davis)** Cofounder at Women-Matter.org S **Weeks Response:** " Thank you for that information"

"The Patrons of Husbandry, also known as The Grange, started in 1875 welcomed women with equal representation and rights." **(Charlie McAlpine)** Boston University **https://en.wikipedia.org/wiki/National Grange of the Order of Patrons of Husbandry** is a site with a great deal of information on this Order.

"Also, there were no "official" Rape Crisis Centers, Domestic Violence Shelters, University Women's Studies Programs & Women's Centers or Ethnic Centers & Ethnic Studies Programs before the 1970's. All were fought hard for & until this day are still challenged to justify their existence. As a former Director of a University Women's Center, I know this first hand and was still surprised how some young women assumed these places had always been around. I am forever grateful to all the dedicated women that came before me & fought so hard for our Equality. It's so important to know our history, especially at this time of dismantling of our rights by this new administration. Thank you for posting this great summary!!" **(Sandrrea Gonzales)**

"Well said. The question is will we, the women of today, stand and be recognized for the women of tomorrow." **(Deborah DiColo)** UniServ Field Rep at NJEA

S Weeks **Response:** "I think that when I read about the women that were thrown in prison and beaten. I don't know if I am that strong."

"Sorry, but a lot of "young women" DO know this. And we're NOT satisfied with the status quo. Did you not notice the amazing age-range in the march photos? I'm tired of getting blamed for being "ignorant" just because of my age. Stop assuming – we're all fighting the same fight here." **(Andrea Weber) S Weeks Response**: "The article was for all women and a lot of young women and older women were not aware of their history. I don't know who blames you for being ignorant, but it certainly wasn't me."

"It is an assault to my intelligence and a disregard for history that we can lose these rights not protected by the constitutional. It is an assault to all those who have given their lives for these rights. If these rights are taken away by these ignorant and backward appointed judges, I only hope that history will show how barbaric they are. How can in this time can someone be "appointed" and take away our rights as women, as homosexuals, as young women, as citizens, as green card holders, as those merely seeking refuge from terror. It is an abomination." **(Elizabeth Prodey)** Adjunct Faculty at Harford Community College

"Marvelous piece so important to inform you women of women's struggle for human rights. I took it upon myself, when as a mature student, I discovered that many of the young women students weren't aware even of the progress made during the sixties. I felt it was my duty to point out that for instance maternity leave was not available when my first child was born and consequently, my job was lost! The young women were shocked as they had taken this right for granted!" **(Deirdre Houston)** IT Sligo, Ireland

"With Trump and Pence, as well as all the people Trump has placed in his administration, we are in danger of losing everything women have been fighting for since before the Civil War." **(Paloma Guerrero)** Polytechnic University of Valencia

"I'm happy for those who have never been discriminated against because of their sex, but let's not pretend that because some women from places were fully empowered to check out books at the local library, that there's never been any such thing as discrimination against women. I've personally never been bothered by poison ivy, but I don't go telling people it doesn't cause a rash." **(Christin O'Cuddehy)** Sacremento, CA

"This is so timely. We lose ground to the Trump administration every day. I think young women who have only known President Obama have not felt the brunt of laws being reversed until now...already the Muslim ban has affected them, climate change data removed from the government sites, and plans for further destruction ahead." **(Simons Lisa)** Berkley, CA

"It should also be mentioned that the ERA was never ratified in the USA. For those of you who never heard of this, Google it. Wikipedia spells out the whole thing. We Canadian women were watching from up north with great hope. In the end, we were lucky that with our Canadian Constitution, still in London at that time, was repatriated by the Prime Minister Trudeau (father) in 1982. That gave us a chance at it without having to go through a cumbersome amending formula. We got it, although not without major hurdles. Section 28 of our Canadian Charter of Rights and Liberties which is part and parcel of our Constitution, spells out equality for men and women, above all other rights guaranteed in the Charter." **(Medeleine Delaney)** Retraitee el benevole

S Weeks Response: "Thanks for your comment. If you go to the end of the article, a paragraph starts with, "Guess What?" and that tells that the ERA was never ratified. Lucky for your Canadian Constitution! My grandmother was born in Quebec and immigrated when she was 8 years old."

"Such a one sided article. Shame on the author." **(Terry Critzer Menendez)** ETSU

"Good summary. I would just like to point out that the landmark US Supreme Court case of Griswold v Connecticut was decided in 1965. Pre-dating Roe v Wade by only 7 years, Griswald was the case that relied on the right to privacy to hold that a state may not criminalize birth control pills. Talk about wiping something away with the swipe of a pen....you will not find a "right to privacy" listed in the Constitution or Bill of Rights. Rather, it is included in the penumbra of rights that we generally associate with liberty, and hence the US Supreme Court read it into the constitution. Strict constructionists (those who say that only rights strictly in enumerated in constitution exist) would like to eliminate the right to privacy. This paves the way for overturn not only of Roe v Wade but also overturn of Griswold v Connecticut and your right to even access birth control. Think twice about that slippery slope." **(Alexandria Broughton Skinner)** Alexandria Skinner, Attorney at Law

S Weeks Response: "Thank you for that information!!

"Thank you Sharon Weeks for your well defined article. I'm 59 years old and did not grow up facing the lack of women's rights. I've always been told that my 'power' is my womanhood and I have never faced an issue where my rights were violated simply because I am female. What you have written is a terrific summary of the struggles women (and other minorities) have suffered and endured throughout history. You are spot on saying young women of today share a 'status quo' of complacency regarding the history of women's and certain minority's hard earned right for basic and simple rights which have been granted just within the last century. Your article deserves front page recognition with intent to grab the attention of many young women to learn more about the battles, lost and won, that allows them to vote, hold positions of power and to be treated equally." **(Deborah Flathers Windhorst) Louisville, Kentucky**

S Weeks Response: "Thanks for your comment, takes the sting out of those who violently or sarcastically disagree!"

"Pardon me, but I think a lot more women do know and understand their rights and responsibilities that your treatise acknowledges. The result, Trump is President." **(Bill McDaniel)** University of Southern California

"In the 1960's my grandmother bought a house and had to put it in her grown son's name because at the time women could not own property in the state of New York. She did this twice – with 2 different male uncles. When they married she gave them the homes. She was poor- and sweet, but couldn't own property in the state she lived in. What a shame." **(Karen Miller)** Director of Services at Beckfield College

"Thank you. I graduated from high school in 1974, it saddens me at the age of 60 that I am still arguing for women's equality. But I won't stop. Thanks again." **(Patricia Hendricks Constantine)** Ferris State University-Kendall College of Art & Design

"Keep fightin the good fight." **(Jeff Bland)**

"Thank you! I fear so much that women will see their rights eroding. You have presented detailed facts and figures that may help all women realize we CANNOT be complacent. I have had young women say that they appreciate all that has been done by women in the past, but there is no need to worry now!! Thanks, again for proving we DO need to worry!" **(Thea Jorgensen**

Whitehead) Professional Mermaid at Weeki Wachee Springs

"But as with all other issues, that was then, this is now, and all that stuff was in my history book. We have to remember this history, but not relive, the only people that are still oppressed are those that keep beating the dead horse." **(Bobbi Lynne Hoover)** Bethlehem Central Senior High School

"Merci" **(Maryse Gerbaud)** La Reorthe, Pays De La Loire, France

"YOU ALL UNDERSTAND SHE STATES FACTS GOING BACK TO 1870, NOT 1970 RIGHT???? Don't be so hellbent on missing the f'ing point!" **(Sheri Bianca Wilson-Edwards)** Burbank, California

"What a crime more than half the population not equal....what happened with the CEDAW (convention to end discrimination against women) at the U.N.? USA failed to ratify." **(Suzia Aufderheide)** SOSC

"Not all women know real freedom. Many first generation European girls – such as myself, fight for their right to choose what is best for them in this country. The glass ceiling isn't glass sometimes, but heavy rock that needs clearing away. The freedom from limitations – for myself I have a constant reminder on my gender, however I will keep battling." **(Merita Hojhali)** CSUSB

"Every woman, man and teenager needs to see "Iron Jawed Angels." Wonderful depiction of what it took to get women the Right to Vote." **(Marianne Brodlo)** Sales at REMAX 440

One Hundred Years Ago this month, August 1920, Women Won the Right to Vote!!

"As a female I have personally experienced life's little slurs. As a married college senior I was over cut in absences and asked for a note from my PARENTS. When informed I was married, they want one from my husband. I could not get a charge account in Macy's in my name, needed my husband's OK. Ever try buying a car while female?? I always vote. Because my grandmother, college educated mother of 11 could not until she was middle aged. When my mother was born women could not vote! It never ends." **(Margaret Magennis Quinn)** St. John's University+

"When I divorced my first husband in 1989 in New York State, I needed his permission in my divorce agreement to return to using my maiden name." **(Kerry Reardon)** University of Delaware

"Men need to remember the struggle also." **(David Baker)**

"This is a very important summary and should be taught in every high school. People have forgotten are just not aware or just never knew. Stop looking at your phones and pay attention. As it is said, "Freedom is NOT

Free." **(Arleen Larzelere)** P.A. at Renee Richards, M.D. PC

"Thank you for this terrific article and the historical perspective! All women and men should read this! Particularly republican women, who for the life of me I don't understand why they would support this administration, but I think you hit the nail on the head, they don't want to rock their safe lives and their "status quo." **(Tracy Diner)** Total Wellness OC

"Imagine. Again, it all boiled down to being.....white....and male!" **(Lynda Musser Belloma)** National Sales Training Manager, Warner Communications NYC

"Everything you listed is very important and honorable and I'm so grateful. However, I am happy with my life as a woman and I don't appreciate being made to feel as I am settling." **(Kathy McCann Paull)** **S Weeks Response**: I am sorry you felt like you were being made to feel like you were settling. That is not the case. The point was to make you aware of how you might lose your happy life. Just be happy, but also aware.

"In 1972, a judge in Frederick County, Maryland, denied my petition to change my name back to my maiden name. My husband even consented, and he went with me to the hearing in the judge's chambers." **(Judith Hoggan)** **S Weeks Response:** "I got mine back in the 70's the same way I changed it. Notified Social Security and the Motor Vehicle Department of a name change!"

"And we still have far to go, young women. Do not give up the fight for progress. Women are second-class citizens all over the world. Patriarchy is not our friend. Keep up the fight, sisterhood!" **(Diane Slagle)** UCSD

"Brava!" **(Jim Reilly)** University of Minnesota

"Women in 2017 continue to be suppressed in a man's world. Subtle discrimination discourages participation at the highest levels of industry and politics. Women are not equally represented in math, engineering and information technology." **(Donna Albert)** Energy Engineer at State of Washington

"We all do tend to take our rights for granted. I like to make another analogy. We all know the horrors of slavery and lingering bigotry which covers all kinds of societal ills, including racism and sexism. With the Emancipation Proclamation slavery ended, and by 1870 the right to vote was granted, at least in theory if not always in practice, to every citizen regardless of color. However, women of any color apparently were not considered to be citizens. As this woman's commentary points out, women continued to be regarded as "property," and treated as such. Now, considering the rampant racism and discrimination both men
(and women of color, notably former black slaves and native (indigenous) Americans continue to suffer, one would think the white wives and daughters of white

64

men would have been given preferential treatment in matters of civil liberties, including the right to vote. But, the fact is, emancipated black male slaves who might barely be able to read or write were granted the right to vote 50 years before any white woman, including highly educated white women with college degrees were granted that right with the ratification of the 15th Amendment in 1920. The Suffragettes who marched, demonstrated and fought for that right were severely beaten, the hair pulled out or cut, humiliated in every manner, and jailed by their white male counterparts who mocked the, force fed them, subjected them to torture, and called them every conceivable name, including anarchists, insane and whores. There may have been deaths – I haven't researched recently in depth. To this day, in 2017, misogyny is very much evident at its very worst and sexism at its more subtle; and both are rampant around the world. It certainly was evident in our last election result. Hillary Clinton was treated in the basest and most insulting manner conceivable, as were Nancy Pelosi, Meagan Kelly, Carly Fiorina and other prominent women in the spotlight. Perhaps the most shocking aspect to me is the willingness with which so many women turn on their sisters to discredit and to destroy them, particularly those women who witlessly and ignorantly enjoy the entitlements others struggled so valiantly and courageously to ensure all women decades before, including the right to assemble and exercise free speech. To have access to birth control and safe abortions. To own and dispose of property in our own name. To marry one another regardless of color without fear of being arrested and thrown into prison. To have equal consideration for the custodial rights to our children. In divorces up to relatively recent times, and in Great Britain at present (as far as I know) women did/do not have that right. And last but not least the right to vote. We still have a long way to go to overcome pervasive sexist attitudes (campus rapes and men like Trump, but he's just the tip of the iceberg) and we could lose it all in a heartbeat. It's is all under siege as we fuss and fume. We must unite and support one another in solidarity. **(Sierra Muse)**

S Weeks Response: I agree with what you say. I had, in the unedited version of this article, stated that black men were given the right to vote before women, but, alas, issues of space kept several things out."

"I just have to tell you Thank you. Thank you. Thank you. Every word, genius. So true...needs to be said over and over and over, until they realize our rights can be taken away (by men) at any time. We can't take them for granted. We can't close our eyes. I'm in CA and ran across this article. The best things I've read since Gloria Steinem. Thank you." **(Heide Guio)**

"Nobody is taking away a woman's right to abortion. The government is simply saying they do not want to pay for it, that is my money and I do not want to pay for it. If you have reproductive Rights you have reproductive responsibilities, they go hand-in-hand. Pay for your own way. Grow up." **Eleanor Vallone)** Associate Broker at Coldwell Banker Realty Assoc. Inc.

"Thanks for saying what needs to be said! History has never been written by women, but their diaries and letters show us their determination to set he records straight." **(Libby Parker)** Menlo-Atherton High School

"Good article. I am upset that so many younger women have fallen back into the mindset that being a "boy toy" makes their lives more meaningful. Makes me feel like I wasted my time so many years ago to make things better for us, was all in vain." **(Miriam Esme Caro)** Retired Registered Nurse

"My husband and I just discussed this hours ago when a bill for the car that I bought on my own arrived in the mail addressed to him." **(Dawn Bashara)** Communications & Development Director/for Neighbors, Nebraska

"Sent this to my daughter and some other young ladies I know." **(Phil Manson)** University of Georgia

"What every mother should tell her daughter. Her husband. And especially her son." **(Nancy Harmon)**

"A visit to the Women's Rights museum in upstate NY was eye opening. It is still legal in some states to rape your wife. Domestic violence is still legal, technically, in a few states. It was stunning to see the state by state comparisons." **(Gail McSweeney Macinnes)** Princetown, New Hampshire

"Excellent points to which I would add a few that are important to young women today to recognize, especially considering they all were in effect during their mothers' lifetimes. Their mothers and grandmothers could not: **1**. Keep her job if she was pregnant. Until the Pregnancy Discrimination Act in 1987, women could be fired from their workplace for being pregnant. **2,** Report cases of sexual harassment in the workplace. The first time that a court recognized sexual harassment in the workplace was in 1977 and it wasn't until 1980 that sexual harassment was officially defined by the Equal Employment Opportunity Commission. **3**. Be acknowledged in the Boston Marathon. Women could not don their running shoes until 1972. **4,** Get a credit card. Until the Equal Credit Opportunity Act in 1974 women were not able to apply for credit. In 1975, the first women's bank was opened. **5**. Refuse to have sex with her husband. The mid 70's saw most states recognize marital rape and in 1993 (YES – IN NINETEEN-NINTY-TWO IT WAS STILL LEGAL FOR A MAN TO RAPE HIS WIFE) it became criminalized in all 50 states. Still, marital rape is often treated differently to other forms of rape in some states even today. (credit to Ms Magazine for excerpts of this list.)" **(Kara Rouker)** Bloomington, Indiana

"Sing it sister!!! Spot on!" **(Judy Shargaa)**

"I carried the ERA petition and was chased by an angry white man down a gravel road who was trying to beat me with a broom....I will always remember the fear. You girls pay attention...I have been successful because of hard work....not equal treatment." **(Jaybird Lambert)** University of Kansas

"Many women are very much aware of the alternate history created by revising textbooks, and also know the facts behind the achievements made to date. This is an excellent article summarizing how far we've come and how much more needs to be achieved. For those who didn't know, I hope it helps to explain why so many women marched." **(Denise Ward)** Member of technical staff at Nokia

"Donald Trump's election should cause all females AND the males who love them to NOT let him take away a single right that exists now. Trump must be watched like a robin with its eye on the worm. Our elected officials must be asked to keep us informed if the Trump administration does even one single thing to undo our rights and our environmental protections. I think that more and more people are starting to understand the danger that he represents. Republicans:

what do YOU want your legacy to be once Trump is no longer your president?" **(Debbie Hinman)** University of New Hampshire

"Very important. I'd love every young and not so young woman to read this. I've lived some of it, and I still learned a lot!" **(Kathy Baskett)** George Washington High School

"I would like to add that during the Suffrage movement, Black women were often excluded, or discouraged from participating. It's important to know the history of racism in the feminist movement, because we need to move past that and work together to insure civil rights for ALL women." https://www.nwhm.org/...rights.../AfricanAmericanwom en.html" **(Leslie Toussaint)** Ellicott City, Maryland

"The State of Florida still will not allow a woman owned S-Corp to purchase real estate, using a bank loan, without her husband's signature. I was amazed!" **(Linda Ackley)** Owner/President at Third Millennium Fine Arta, Inc.

"Thanks for the concise, if horrifying, history. Honestly, I lived through some of this and I still cannot believe we are so slow in correcting the long list of injustices pertaining to women's rights. We must not go backward on this." **(David Gibson)** Queen's University

"Women, had they been aware of this history, with just a few more of them bothering to vote in their best interests, could have prevented this disaster of a US election" **(Dixie Hayduk)**

"I so hope your rights will be ensured in your constitution some day. In Canada we attained this in 1982...1400 of us, representing millions, went to parliament to insure the equality clause in our Charter of Rights and Freedoms. It is our back up as we work for equality of opportunity for all." **(Bev LeFrancois)** Self-Employed

"I respect your opinion greatly. Yet, as a young woman of 35 years old, I have to disagree with you about the young women being "complacent" and being comfortable with our lives. I worked at Planned Parenthood and after the election we saw a huge increase in women choosing to change to a long acting birth control for the only reason they thought they were going to lose it. We are well aware of what happened before us and we are very afraid for what our daughters may have to endure. Every woman in every generation had their fights. It's also so important to remember that along every step there were women who did not support the advance in women's rights. I understand the frustration, but blaming young women who really are trying in their own way to change the world to better their life isn't going to make them more involved. It will only alienate them and you will lose supporters." **(Sare Thielen)** Eau Claire, Wisconsin

"A very good summary of how we got here. I am struck by the number of "that didn't happen to me" comments seeking to cast doubt on the narrative. A gentle reminder that just because it didn't happen to you, doesn't mean it didn't happen. That these laws limiting women's freedoms were in place is a matter of historical, legislative, provable fact." **(Esther Po)**

"This article is a great reminder of what there is both to lose and to gain. As I read the comments, my real fear is not CWMs, Trump, or even global warming. It is the missed change for women in North America to unite, take charge, and ensure a future for our children and grandchildren. Take the power ladies and sort out the details later. Look to Iceland and Sweden to see what women in legislative power can do to heal the greed of capitalist patriotism." **(Kyra Garson)** Simon Fraser University

"I am embarrassed that I didn't know some of this. But then, as the author notes, the textbook industry is controlled by a few. How do we change that?" **(Gregory Gaiser)** Trainer at Hakomi Institute Southwest

"Wiped away with the swipe of a pen" or is it an inked phallus?" **(Laura Priebe)**

"So now that you have itemized all the wrongs that have been righted....what are you still bitching about?" **(Bob Adams)** Hendersonville, Tennessee

"So true. Women's rights are not just for women – they are human rights for everyone and must be supported for a truly democratic society." **(Brian Margaret Grant)** St-Laurent

"My mother was born when women weren't allowed to vote. In 1965, I was denied car insurance from All State Insurance because I was recently divorced, although my husband got to keep his. I was told by my agent women were too emotional to drive. Now we have a President who believes in grabbing women by the pussy. My daughter, who is a millennial, worked hard for Hillary, but all young girls need to protect their rights." **(Barbara Mclane)** University of Utah, graduated in 1988

"When we married, Dan and I lived frugally so we could save my teaching salary. We bought a stock with it that luckily doubled in value. It was the down payment on a home that we both worked on to improve, selling it at a profit. We did the same thing again, and put that money on a house in Atlanta. The state of Georgia required Dan to sign an agreement that he was "giving" me equal rights to ownership of the Atlanta house "in return for love and devotion." Only he was assumed to have a right to ownership. My share was to be considered a gift from him." **(Margaret Curtis)** Atlanta, GA

"It was a nice history lesson on the white woman's fight for equality in American. One bit of proof that this article is for white women and their struggles is when the author said blacks gained the right to vote, implying that brown women were included in the right to vote which we know is not accurate. I used to ascribe to feminist views but do not anymore as I see that it is singularly focused on white women and their issues. My daughter attended the women's march and came away with the same thoughts. I know people will get upset and defensive when reading my comment. Get defensive if you will, but my comments are coming from a place of my own personal experiences with the women's movement. And getting defensive and upset about my personal experiences as opposed to listening is the reason I have disengaged from this movement." **(Kharmen Dixon)**

Response S Weeks: "I think I understand what you are saying. It was from the comments of some young white women that began my writing. It was not an intentional effort to exclude anyone. I think the struggle for the rights that I mentioned is twice as hard for women of color."

"I know many of my friends think I am over-zealous with my liberal views. I admit, I am just that. This is just one of the things that have shaped my view. The destruction part now in power is attempting to destroy women's rights as well as most other social reforms that have been fought for and won over the years. Health care, veterans care, education, care of the environment, workers rights, as well as many other issues are on the chopping block. If people sit back and think that it doesn't matter to you who is elected, these things will

happen because the destruction part will win." **(Gary Swart)** Central Washington University
S Weeks Response: "Thank you for your comments!"

"You might be interested in: <u>Assigned by the US Government</u>, in 1946, Gen. MacArthur, then head of the Japanese Occupation Authority, was given the task of writing a constitution for Japan. He assigned the task to a 22 year old naturalized American citizen, Beate Sirota Gordon. She was told to use the US Constitution as a model. She did, but she added two striking simple but powerful clauses into the modern Japanese Constitution. These clauses stipulate equality among the sexes as well as civil rights for women involving marriage, money and family. Never widely known in her home country she later became a well-known, decorated figure in Japan for her path-breaking efforts. In other words: the Japanese Constitution has an equal rights clause. Ours does not, despite mighty effort to introduce one." **(Sue J. Acocks)** Ferris State University

"Yes, it is STILL a white man's World and getting more and more violent, toxic and deadly by the day......"WE ALL DO BETTER WHEN WE ALL DO BETTER!" Senator Paul Wellstone, MN (My senator and they killed him, too.)" **(Dee Ann Greenlaw Royce)** Teacher, retired.

"Let's not forget that Native Americans were not given US citizenship until 1924 and were prohibited from voting in many states until 1957." **(Vance McMillan)** Air Force Institute of Technology

"This is an excellent article except for one mistake: Not all states have equal rights for women written in their constitution. Here is a quickie list at the bottom of the wicki definition. Do you know if your state has equal rights for women in their constitution? Oregon doesn't. This is a big conversation." https://en.wikipedia.org/wiki/State_Equal_Rights_Amendments **(Anastasia Miller)** Olympia, Oregon

"Wow! The Equal Rights Amendment was never ratified? That did not dawn on me that there is no amendment for that!! So it was only Title IX that gave women access to colleges, universities and military academies and not the ERA? I feel that this will not be solved or even brought up during this administration." **(Peter McClain)** Retired Military

"Thank you, thank you! Both before and after the election I have had conversations with a number of young women who have absolutely no sense of civic responsibility. They have no knowledge or appreciate for the battles that have been fought on their behalf. They take their rights and citizenship totally for granted. It is very disappointing. Actually, I am outraged. I am going to print this out and mail it to a number of young women." **(Jean Cunningham)** University of St. Thomas

"My mom's a fundamentalist Christian. She holds the standard literalist interpretation of the Bible with respect to women. For decades, I've pointed out that much of what she takes for granted now is due to feminists throughout our history who opened up possibilities for our lives as women. I tell her that, even as she casts her conservative vote on election days, she owes a debt of gratitude to the women who fought for her right to vote. I've never had an effect on changing her beliefs, but she is unsettled by the thought." **(Michelle LaRocque)**

"Thank you for your summary. So many young women today are basking beside their pools of complacency, and pointing fingers at the feminist mean and women who fought for their right to do so. I try hard not to condemn this kind of cowardice, but there are times when I feel that these "self-satisfied, entitled little drones" do not deserve the rights that we fought so hard for. Please forgive this outburst, but I see this every day among so many of the young women in ordinary day-to-day contact and in the increasing tendency to "bully" other young women who are not in their own social or religious circles." **(Orpha Barry)** SFSU

"Reading through some of the comments on this great article, I noticed very few men have posted a reaction or are showing their support. That's disturbing, in many ways.....This story clearly is about human rights in the first place, and certainly all about men and their behavior through history." **(Hend Berkelaar)** Kwaliteitsmanager at Gebrema B.V. (Netherlands)

"This is really great and very well thought. I appreciate your post immensely! Your words are very motivational and timely as we all are having to fight to keep what is good in the world right now with this administration and Congress, it would seem. However, maybe I can offer some words of encouragement here. I was reading this article out loud to my 13 year old son who is in 8th grade and he told me he has learned quite a bit about women's rights in his middle school. He said he's studied women's history with regard to suffrage rights and ownership rights as well as the fact that women had very little rights and "say" over their own lives at an earlier time, not so long ago in history. I was extremely happy to hear this, of course, because he had not mentioned it before. I'm sure this information is available in the schools because of these battles throughout history by others who fought to make it so." **(Julie Landoll Henerson)** Hospice RN Case Manager, Ohio Living Home Health & Hospice

"Thank you for your eloquent and beautiful summary. We won't stop fighting, and defeat is not an option." **(Abby Schwarz)** Massachusetts Institute of Technology

"Let's be VERY CLEAR ladies. Rights are not Rights if some asshat who doesn't agree with you can erase them with the stroke of a pen. They are privileges. Don't agree? Think they are God given? If that's the case, then why did our so called GOD given rights have to be changed so many times, why did we only have them when other countries had 13, 29, and some not at all? Why did one of our so called Rights have to do with liquor and promptly get changed? Did God miss

His Holy Highball? NO, we made it all up. These aren't rights. They're privileges, and as privileges they are about as solid as AIR. Which is why they are disappearing as fast as you can say racist misogynist president and too many of his cohorts. Not just here. All over Europe, too, which is where I currently am. Got a guy in the Oval Office who hates women? What the hell do you think is going to happen to your precious Rights? Right this way, ladies, down the toilet. Wake up. Nothing is God given. That's the argument of the person who has no other logic to lean on. Until something is LAW it is nothing. And as we see, laws that we fought for (I'm 64) are under fire. Nothing is for granted. Nothing is sacred. Nothing is God given except your life. What you do with it – whether you stand up for what you think is right, the privilege to own and manage your own body, and live your own life, is up to you. We ARE losing it all. All you have to do is see who's in the henhouse. Old white males who make comments in all their breathtaking heartbreaking ignorance – that women don't need healthcare below the belt after fifty. Well, how bout we inform Mr. Man he doesn't need his penis after fifty? How about that God given privilege? Just saying." **(Julia E. Hubbel)** President at WordFood

"It has been stated...."women shall inherit the world"....your day is coming." **(Scott Brodrick)** Wolfeboro, New Hampshire

"Ken Burns' "Not for Ourselves Alone" is a terrific movie on the women's rights movement. All

Americans should see it. Point to ponder......Even our movement
for equality is told by men............"**(Lyn Des Marais)**
Legislative Director at Vermont Farm Bureau
S Weeks Response: "Thank you for that, will get the movie."

"I'm saddened and ashamed by how many comments I had to scroll down before I saw a response to this by another man. As a teacher, I continue to be astonished at just how much young Americans do NOT know about their past and the struggles that won them their "status quo"; the only thing missing from Sharon Weeks' stirring narrative is a parallel history of the labor movement, a history which has also been effaced by the rightwing appropriation of history." **(David Pringle)** Temple Terrace, Florida
S Weeks Response: "Thanks for those remarks. The original article was printed in a newspaper and they have size limits. I had to edit quite a bit before it was printed. You are right, and the labor movement is taking major hits."

"Women were also not allowed to be jurors until 1973!! Never forget, it says "all men are created equal." Thank you for this article. **(Faye Cragin)** Plymouth State University

---

1975 Taylor v. Louisiana, 419 U.S. 125 (1976) denies states the right to exclude women from juries.

"Yup, and equality remains an illusion here in Australia with women dying unprotected from domestic violence, no parity in pay scales in many industries, poorly funded child care, etc. etc. If we accept a low bar, that is what we are going to get!"

(Gail Bateman) Appollo Bay, Victoria, Australia

"Preach it, sister! At 70, I tell young women this hard truth all the time. If YOU aren't a feminist, the least you can do is thank one!!" **(Ann Hobbs)** Foster/Adopt Caseworker retired, TX Dept Family Protective Services

S Weeks Response: "Wonderful idea!!"

"As a child of the 60's when the Women's Equal Rights and the feminist movement were strong, we had leaders like **Betty Friedan, Billie Jean King, Gloria Steinem, Eleanor Roosevelt and Odetta Holmes**, who fought for not only women's rights, but for the rights of everyone to be treated equally. It is so sad to see that we woman are still struggling for those rights after all the sacrifices many have made to get us this far. We must keep up the fight." **(Kathleen Tomasik Panasiewicz)**

"Until reading Sharon Weeks' essay I had forgotten about the restrictions I faced when purchasing my 1st car, obtaining a credit card in my name only, being asked on a job interview if I had or planned to have children, not going to college because I believed my only options were to be either a teacher of a nurse. My parents encouraged my brother to seek a higher

81

education, but felt my future should be getting married and having children, in other words, to become a "housewife." It was mandatory then in middle school to take Home Economics which consisted in a semester of learning a pittance about cooking and another semester of sewing. The first project was making a gathered skirt which included a zipper or in those days called a placket. I graduated from high school in 1958 so it was not all that long ago. Oh, also, competitive sports were not in the curriculum for young women." (**Mary Strickler**)

"....and the white supremist men in Washington are just the sort to screw it all up, let us not forget what the white men have done to the American Indians in the past, and now currently taking their treaty land away under the guise of eminent domain.". (**Vicki Walbert**) Anoka Ramsey
S Weeks Response: "Good Points!"

"A female still could not buy a house in 1950. I bought my first house single 21 years of age late 60's and the bank pres could not figure out why I would want to. Also asked WHAT IF YOU GET PG? I said, "Won't be yours!" I got the loan. In Miami, FL" (**Sue Harrison**) Mt. Carmel High School
S Weeks Response: "What a fantastic response! Thanks!"

"I have six daughters and you are right, but remember, nowhere else in the world do men and women have it so good." (Ralph Moerschbacher) Jersey Shore,

Pennsylvania
S Weeks Response: "I think they do in Scandinavia."

"Thank you for the reminder to young women. Being 75, I remember very well." **(Kathryn Honeycutt)** Vassar College, Bard College, US-Madison, NCSU

"Well said. The rights won are only still there because every day women fight to keep them. If we let our collective guard down, these rights will be stripped away, and anyone who doesn't acknowledge that is either ignorant or a fool. There is never a better time to be vigilant than NOW. And the only way to achieve our goals is to STICK TOGETHER!" **(Naomi Cartledge)** St. Mary's Star of the Sea Catholic College.

"...reminding us once again, though women and African Americans have made great strides in the last 50+/- years we still have a long way to go before equality is reached. Look no further than our local and national political representation. Women and other minorities are still woefully under represented." **(Cindy Hemenway)** Boston State College

"So does that mean that our Muslin brothers are not leading a life of equal rights for everyone! We should all be good Christians and just allow them in the neighborhood right! Sure they'll adjust! Let me know so I CAN be prepared AND HELP THEM GET THEIR ADJUSTMENT." **(Joseph Digiro)** Berklee College of Music

"Very concise. I might add, when I was first married in 1966 I realized I had no credit in my name, I couldn't open a bank account or buy a car or even register a car in my own name. I marched to change all that. However, no amount of marching or phone calls could help us pass the ERA-Equal Rights Amendment. To this day we have not be granted EQUAL RIGHTS UNDER THE CONSTITUTION!!!! To me, that is abominable". **(Ginny Villafranca)** Wayne, New Jersey

"There are a lot of people in this country who think only rich white men should rule this nation. These people in charge now have proven that they will stoop to new lows to keep control of the money. If women somehow threaten their ideals and don't pay attention to what they're doing we're going to end up back in the 50's." **(Jane Berresord)**

"Equal rights for others doesn't mean less rights for you. It's not pie. Equal rights, (to me), is effectively like sunshine–we should all stand in it and feel the same warmth." **(Jason Zandri)** Sr. Cloud Infrastructure Consultant at Tallan

"It's incredible to see it all laid out in front of you like this! In the 70's my mother worked and saved money to buy a car. She took me to San Jose, a city an hour away, to look. She picked out the one she wanted, but when she went to purchase it, they weren't going to let her without her husband there to show that she had her husband's permission. I have never seen my mother so livid in my life? We drove away in the car." **(JoAnne McInstire)** Grass Valley, California

" ....pay attention, please, lest you lose it all. Lest we all lose it all." And men lose it all, too. We're not stronger when not equal. Each person should have the right to gain their true purpose and potential in life without discrimination." **(Mark Bell)** Righter at Technically Write
Response S Weeks: "Thank you for your comments."

"And just in the last couple of decades, the state or municipality can bring battery charges against a domestic abuser, negating the need for the victim to formally press charge. Male against female is the most common, however, many other types exist. This only because women fought for it." **(Peg Johnson)** Chicago, IL

"Not only an American summary, but worldwide we have the same issues. May I remind women (as I do with my daughter and grand-daughter) that their fight is endless and mine as well, because I am not only a man, but a human being." **(Christian Nittis)**

"I am 78. I got my first credit card (Mobil) when I was in my early 20's. When I got married and changed my last name (which was what people did then), Mobil changed the account to my new husband's name, without my permission. When we applied for a mortgage several years later (around 1970), I was teaching and we had one child. We were in the process of completing our family by adopting our second child, Rick. The banks in our town refused to include my income in determining whether we qualified for a loan; they said that was because I was still fertile (now, how would they know that?) and could get pregnant and lose my job or decide to quit working. In the phone directory for the school where I taught, I was listed as "Mrs. Irwin Beitch", even though my husband had nothing to do with my teaching there. It took a battle to get that changed to my own name, and another battle to get my title changed from "Mrs." To "Dr." in the directory. In 1978 my husband and I applied for passports, to go to Europe. We were given one passport with both of our photos, with my husband's name on it; that was apparently how things were done then. When Irwin died, I had to jump through hoops and present notarized death certificates numerous times, to get credit cards and utilities changed to my name (particularly ironic, since I had been the chief bill payer for the 47 years of our marriage). Next, it was only recently in history that a husband and wife could list both names in a phone directory, for a shared land phone; the first 30 years or so of my marriage to Irwin (before cell phone had been invented and before there was an internet), I could not list my name in the phone directory (and therefore, old friends could not even find me if they needed to contact me). Another inequality is that even today, when service people call the house, they assume that my husband is the head of household and that I have my husband's last name (which I do not; we were married almost 5 years ago, and each of us kept our own last name). They ask to speak with my husband, even though in some cases I was the one who originally contacted the service person or company. We women may have come a long way, but we are not there yet, and some of the rights for which we have fought could be lost at the flourish of a Presidential pen. We who care about rights of women and other marginalized groups should not let ourselves become too complacent." **(Barbara Rose Beitch)** Basic Eye Research, currently a docent at Yale University **S Weeks Response:** "Thank you so much for your comments!"

"Oh, my. I remember some of these discriminations. This is a trip down memory lane and a sense of gratitude that I owe nothing to any man." **(Kay Duren)** Fair Oak, California

"Complacency is like cancer...people, standing against these injustices is the only cure..! Women of the world unite...!!!" **(Genevieve Grant)** Monash University

"This is interesting but incomplete. Check it out. Wyoming's records on the advances made for women's rights including the right to vote in 1870 as it came into statehood. First woman governor, all women city government, etc., etc." **(Jan Vacha Caldwell)** Phoenix, AZ

1870 The first sexually integrated grand jury hears cases in Cheyenne, Wyoming. The chief justice stops a motion to prohibit the integration of the jury, stating: "It seems to be eminently proper for women

---

> to sit upon **Grand Juries, which will give them the**
> **best possible opportunities to aid in suppressing the**
> **dens of infamy witch curse the country."**

"It seems that since the 1960's some things have not changed – still no equal rights amendment and no equal wages – women are more educated (no more education gap between men and women) and we are a majority in the population. Some fields, such as technology, with the exception of a handful of companies, are still being run by a good old boy system that is inhospitable for women to work in. Women are the hidden asset few companies recognize will make them more profitable if paid an equal wage." **(Frances Beckman)** Retired

"A minor version of this: My sister had a paper route in the 60's when she was a teenager. Someone complained, only because she was a girl and they took it away from her." **(Elizabeth Briars)** Fine Arts Teacher, Artist, Illustrator, taught at Liverpool High School

"I remember when my mother, a college professor, was not allowed to inherit the family property in Texas, it had to be owned by my dad. Not a good moment in time. We have come a long way. That being said, I could do without "pussy" hats and women dressed up as vaginas. It only demeans us and seems to have no purpose but to make us look the fool."
(Mary Lou Johnson) Luther Collect

"Don't forget the **VAWA – Violence Against Women Act** – also in danger." **(Mary Kay Rehard)**

The Violence Against Women Act, established in 1994, was allowed to expire this year - 2020

"Wonderful summation of our women's history. Hope this is something every woman reads. We were once owned by our fathers then, when married, by our husbands." **(Nancy Straub)** Saratoga Springs, New York

"Thank you. It is what I have been saying, but you did it so much more eloquently. I am old enough to remember many of these fights, plus I am a living historian and have the knowledge of others. As a mother of daughters and with granddaughters we cannot let old white men turn back time to "better times" because all that means is better for them." **(Linda L. Wetter)** Aquatic Exercise Instructor, Portland Parks and Recreation

"I would like to add one more thing to this list. When I was in the Navy in the late 60', if you got pregnant (married or not) you were honorably discharged from the service. No military careers for mothers. One Navy nurse took them to court to say they didn't discharge men who had children." **(Kathryn Burks)**

"Expatriation act of 1907 where if a woman was a citizen of the US married a non-citizen, she then lost her citizenship. If a man married a non-citizen she was considered a citizen. So citizenship could only be taken away from a female for the exact same action as a man. In 1915 this law was challenged but was upheld by the Supreme Court in1915." **(Jodi Graves)** Odon High School

" .....in the 1870's women could not own property, could not sign contracts, could not vote, file law suits, nor have their own money. Under their father's roof, he had control and that control was passed to her husband upon marriage. A woman running away from violent domestic abuse was hunted down by the law and returned to her husband as she was his property." Intersectionally speaking, disable women still do not have these rights." **(Hilary Krzywkowski)** Cleveland Heights, Ohio

"Thank you for doing this. I speak about women's rights in the workplace to my daughter and her friends all the time! You live in a beautiful place. I spent my summers as a kid up north near Spooner." **(Joanne Allen-Walker)**
S Weeks Response: "It is beautiful, but that is changing. Sand mines/plants are dotting the landscape. If you drove up Hwy 53 toward Spooner you would be horrified at what has happened to the landscape."

"Marched for the woman's right in 1972 on the streets 'of Paris....shocked to learn that French woman did not have the right to have her own bank account without her husband's signature....that was my first eye opening experience...." **(Sachiko Chiba Reis`)**

"Excellent! I will share and encourage others to pass this on. It was 1961 and I was age 20, married, with a small child. I needed (elective) surgery; my husband was not yet 21. The local hospital tried to pressure me to get my parent's permission for the surgery, since we both were "minors". They also remarked that it was too bad that husband was 3 months short of being 21, since HE was the head of household and could make the decisions. I never forgot how humiliating it was." **(Susan Bidwell-Williams)** Retired

"Please read! Find a way to help prevent your civil liberties from being taken from you. I can't imagine this is not affecting you in some way. If you're male think of your wife, mother, grandmother, daughters or granddaughters, nieces, cousins. Somehow it will impact you in a negative way. Please step up and step out. I'm not able to march but I promise I'll find some way to help prevent the loss of liberties my ancestors and yours fought for. This isn't about your skin color, race, sexual orientation or any negative thoughts or issues. It's about human suffering, pain, neglect, control, from the few over the many. Reading this overwhelmed me. I hope it does the same to you. It's truly an eye opener." **(Shan Thomas)** El Centro College

"Glad to see this brought to light. For so long even former slaves had more guaranteed rights than women!" **(Larry Evans)** Offender Rehabilitation Coordinator specializing in mentally ill, chemically addicted inmates in super max custody, NY State Dept O

"The attitude that "I've never had any trouble with/getting/doing" is fleeting. We are seeing ALEC/Koch writing laws introduced all over the place attempting to "deconstruct" civil rights. It is happening now. One little shove backward at a time. I fought the work place fights for 30 years. If young women don't want to take the time to learn the pitfalls and dangers ahead for trying to maintain legislative rights that can be repealed in a flash and fight to keep it from happening by pushing for an Equal Rights Amendment to engrave Constitutional protection of civil rights to women, they and their daughters stand to lose much. Women's rights are human rights. They can only be insured when made part of our Constitution." **(Lee H. Sisk)**

"I'm happy with all the freedoms I have." **(Ann Wightman)** Cal Poly Pomona **S Weeks Response:** "I am happy that you are. You can tell from other comments that there are many women willing to fight so that you can keep your freedoms."

"In Ireland, a woman could not get a library card without her husband's or father's written permission, up until 1978. Religion has an awful lot to do with the position of women in society." **(Dennis J. O'Connor)**

"An urgent insistent plea to continue to pay close attention, to keep our eyes on the prize in spite of horrible setbacks. "Selective" history benefits only those who choose to keep blinders on; the proclaimed ones in power who believe their blighted ideas are the only ones worthy of lawful protection. It's a marathon for humanity, for decency and full equality. Every sprint forward, every effort, counts. Change is bloody and meets cruelty, ignorance, violence head on. To give up is to allow the continuation of limited, very limited, perspectives." **(Marcie Feldman)** School of the Museum of Fine Arts, Boston

"Lately, I have also been thinking we failed our younger people, by not telling them how bad it was. I suppose we thought they would just know. Civil rights, women's rights, human rights, children's rights, but we must include the ecology. We think they knew how bad it was, turns out they don't. They were not there. I am guilty of not telling them. I regret not telling them. We can't change the past, so we must change the future." **(Annie Eash)** Perdue University

"Thank you for telling again the facts of how we are where we are today and how, with the swipe of a pen, which seems to occur daily, our rights COULD be taken away. It just gets me so upset to hear young women say they don't like to be called feminists because it has negative connotations. Let's see how they would like to be told they couldn't have a job they were more than qualified because they were getting married which would mean they would eventually have children. Or be groped by bosses and have no recourse. Why haven't their mothers drilled it into them to be feminists? One woman in her 40's told me once after talking about feminism years ago, "we rode in on your coattails." It's about time all women fight for the ERA! I can't believe we're still for this! So thank you for this article to remind us all of the struggle." **(Ronnie Teitler Davis) Owner**, Longstream Coaching and Training LLC

"Embarrassing. There is no movement towards "reversal" of LGBT rights. If you were a history teacher, you're certainly cherry-picking. Read Bernard Nathanson's writings on how Jane Roe and the public were manipulated. He was one of the founders of NARAL who later, rightly, became anti-abortion." **(Thomas Lardner)** Wright State University

"Phenomenal summary. Very important. Very well-written. I hold a degree in US History and always had my students look at these issues in an age appropriate context. Many were incredulous that my Mom's dear friend, a WWII veteran with a Purple Heart for horrific injuries sustained when the hospital ship on which she was serving was kamikazed in the So. Pacific just weeks before VJ Day, was denied her Cal. Vet Loan benefit to buy a house in her hometown of Fresno. Why? SHE WAS A WOMAN, UNATTACHED TO ANY MAN. Never married. Father deceased. The year was 1955. Helen had a great job as a nurse in SF. Went home to Fresno as often as possible. Wanted a real home for her aging Mother, an Armenian immigrant who had fled her home country when violent hostilities erupted there in the early 1900's. This denial of veteran benefits happened in MY LIFETIME. Never forget the struggle for equality for ALL continues and

94

demands of each of us constant vigilance!" **(Cathleen A. Gutherie)** San Francisco State University

"Seriously? All of these differences in rights of women and men were years to decades, even centuries ago. Nothing is different today. If you want the best job, get the best education, and work for it. Stop complaining like a woman, stop thinking if you celebrate a random day by not going to work, it will accomplish anything but reinforce the ideas of those who think women are inferior. You want to be equal? Act like an equal!" **(Karen Purdy)** Brownsburg, Indiana
S Weeks Response: "And just who was complaining? Listing the obstacles women have overcome in the last century and asking them to be vigilant so those things are not lost is not complaining. It is educating."

"As much as Supreme Court decisions are venerated and respected, it is clear that they don't always get it right. The dreaded Dred Scott decision is one; the issue of the 1875 decision concerning women's rights is another. It is possible that history will find a few more bad decisions made in more recent times will come to light and be reversed, too."
(Douglas Alan) Columbia, South Carolina

"It should also be mentioned that the ERA, the Equal Rights Amendment was never ratified in the USA. For those of you who never heard of this, Google it. Wikipedia spells out the whole thing. We Canadian women were watching from up north with great hope. In the end, we were lucky that with our Canadian

Constitution, still in London at that time, was repatriated by Prime Minister Trudeau (father) in 1982. That gave us a chance at it without having to go through a cumbersome Amending formula. We got it, although not without major hurdles. Section 28 of our Canadian Charter of Rights and Liberties which is part and parcel of our Constitution, spells out equality for men and women, above all other rights guaranteed in the Charter" **(a)** Works at Retrai'tee et benevole

S Weeks Response: "Thank you for your comments. If you go to the end of the article, a paragraph starts with, "Guess What?" and that tells that the ERA was never ratified. Lucky for your Canadian Constitution.

"At 24 years old, I was not able to get a checking or savings account in the city of Philadelphia. I had moved to the city to start a new job in a non-profit organization. The year is 1984. Even with a payroll check in hand, I was not able to open an account. I had a checking account when I was 16, back in Maine, but the savings account was started by my parents when I was quite young. Back to 1984. After a month with two payroll checks, my boss had received permission from one of our volunteers (who sat on the non-profit board and worked in management at the bank) that I was granted a checking account only. I'm 24 years old, going to the bank with my boss in tow. I was told by my boss, don't you go bankrupt on this account (because of the volunteer: man, who had approved the opening of the checking accounts). I had been on my own for over 4 years and still felt the sting). Thank you, Ms. Weeks, for your quick history lesson. Women today must know that for every position they achieve today, there were at least 10 women (of the recent past) who went before them and their ride was met with emotional, physical, economic and sexual abuse. Yet women of old (50+ years and older) did what we did because of they who came after us – women and men, to educate them along their way." **(Regina McTeague)** Jo-Ann Fabrics and Craft Store

"Hell will freeze over before I ran around like an idiot with a vagina on my head." **(Jean Kern)** Self Employed **S Weeks Response:** "The people who did that didn't do the march any favors (in my opinion) and really distracted from the hundreds of thousands of women, their husbands and fathers who marched."

"Wow. I marched in the 70's and I am just learning some of this history. And, I did know, but had forgotten till now, how fragile our rights as women are." **(Marth Hernandez)** Psychotherapist, Private Practice

"We do need to be reminded of Her-story, and we must become aware that the freedom we North American women now enjoy is not enjoyed globally by our sisters. Some women, in some cultures are still treated as "property", some are denied education, some ritually mutilated, many have no right to vote, work, or do anything to improve their lot in life. It is wonderful that our daughters enjoy some taste of freedom and equality – it is vital that we continue to work toward equal human rights for all. **(Mary Cheney)** Whitehorse, Yukon Territory

"In the 1960's my husband was able to take money out of an account paid by deduction from my check at my credit union. I couldn't take money out of my account without his signature. I closed the account. When we divorced our joint credit cards were closed to me. He still had the accounts. Although our joint credit was based on my credit when we married, when we divorced I had no credit." **(Marty Flint)** Oakdale Joint Union High Alternative School

S Weeks Response: "I am hearing this time and time again."

"Coming late to the discussion, but wanted to add: in 1965 my mother, recently divorced, tried to apply for a Sears credit card. She was denied on the basis that she had no husband. For the rest of her life she used her mother's Sears credit card when she needed to purchase items from Sears. The ironic part is that her mother – my grandmother-never worked a day in her life at a paying job – but because she was married, she was considered a good credit risk. My mother earned a paycheck in her own name, but the sin of not having a husband disqualified her. Years later, when Sears offered her a card in her own name, she refused to take it and continued using grandmom's Sears card. I closed my grandmother's Sears account after my mother died at age 82. We've come a long way, ladies. The fact that some of us didn't encounter this discrimination doesn't minimize what happened to those who did." **(Susan Edelman)** Temple University

"It's the young women in my life who are the strongest feminists. I wonder what young women she's talking about." **(Andromeda Drake)** L.V. Rogers Secondary School
S Weeks Response: "The young women who don't know the history. Many do, but there are also many who don't."

"Men RULE, Women are subservient to MEN. You women should worship men or at least Republican MEN. Dumb asses!" **(Douglas Dameron)** Owner at Douglas Electric

"In 1900 there were no child labor laws. Little girls worked in the New England textile mills starting at age nine for microscopic wages six days a week up to 14 hours a day with n safety equipment or proper ventilation. Their average life expectancy was 25." **(John Geoghegan)** Laguana Niguel, CA
S Weeks Response: "Hard to imagine today, but it still happens in other countries. Thanks for your comments."

"Women position is one of adults when US spread democracy with bombs in East. US have a lot of work to implement democracy on own territory. No time for other countries, despite reward in control of other (mostly east) countries and oil" **(Perla Grass)** . Tehnicki skolski centar Ruder Boskovic

"Wonderful summary. I was honored to work on the Civil rights and WLM movements in the 60's, 70's and beyond. Every generation has to fight against since racism, sexist, able-ism, homophobia, Trans hate, and all their cousins, are alive and well and born into the primitive fears that are so readily manipulated. I worked in abortion rights, day care, employment discrimination, ERA ratification, black political work, and domestic violence. Then I took a breath in my 50's. I was amazed at the change over time. Young women friends responded to my stories of circumstances when I came of age as if they were from two centuries ago and not infrequently people commented that we had come too far for all this to be undone. Nope. During the time of the Women's March, I saw a cartoon that said it all – an elderly woman marcher with a sign that said, "SAME SHIT – DIFFERENT CENTURY." **(Linda Strothman)** Private Practice Psychotherapy

"But you have to ask yourself whether women are actually happier today. So many single mothers struggling, so many searching for commitment in relationships and not finding, so many feeling they need to compete and hate men but still have lots of sex, too many working in dead-end jobs and paying others to do the dead-end job of caring for their kids. It's not insulting your equality when a guy holds the door, buys you flowers, loves your kids as much as you do. Is it a secret dream for you to be happily faithfully married to a good man, cooperatively caring for your family and finding joy in service each other? Throw away the marching shoes and vagina hats and just be a nice person, not an angry feminist! **(Donna Eliason)** Calgary, Alberta

Sharon Weeks: "Didn't respond, but should have on so many levels."

"This is a great read. For all women, young and old, for our young children who have not been exposed to this bit of information, please have them read this! Bravo to this terrific woman to again remind us we must keep on fighting. Like Hillary keeps telling us, "Human rights are women's rights, and women's rights are human rights", once and for all!!!"
(Terri Valensuela)

"Every woman should read this. It sickens me that we have a president proud of his sexual abuse of women. What fresh hell do we have to look forward to. I'm old enough to remember when it was normal for a male boss to put his hands on me and it meant my job if I complained. I, for one am sick of this pretend equality." **(Donna Hensley)** St. Louis, Missouri

"This is American history, but Canada usually is not far behind. Many women don't have these rights and there are those in Canada who would like to enforce law from other cultures that reverse these. Wake up Canada!"
(Judy Saxby) University of Alberta

"Thank you for sharing very important history of Human Rights issues that need to be protected!!! The oldest Women's organization in the United States, 1893, is NATIONAL COUNCIL OF JEWISH WOMEN. This organization works to make sure women, girls, families are protected. Currently,

SFCAHT, SAN FRANCISCO COLLABORATIVE AGAINST HUMAN TRAFFICKING, is working to rescue and protect girls that get trapped in the Sex Trafficking in this country and other countries trap girls, women and boys and men in the Slave Trade! Contact your local NCJW, NcJWSF Section to help all those who have been trapped and could be living next door to you and you don't know it." **(Sandra Gordon)** Daly City, California

"The women that are commenting here that they had no problem getting credit, a library card, a driver's license, whatever when they were younger – Are you saying is that it wasn't a problem for you so you doubt it was a problem for anyone? Or maybe that people who couldn't get credit, it was their fault? Maybe there were pockets of locations (like big cities with liberal lending practices) where you were fortunate; however, the laws weren't on your side and claiming it was "not a problem" does not change that. For many, it WAS a problem and that problem was perfectly legal until someone stood up to change it. BTW I knew someone in the late 80's/early 90's who married, bought a house, and had the marriage annulled because it was easier to purchase a home as a married woman than as a single one. I also bought a home around that time as a single mother. I never thought it was her problem that the process was easier and cheaper if she were married. **(Christine Ballinger)**

"Sexual equality is protected under the Constitution. It's called the Equal Protection Clause." **(Richard Bennett)** Business Attorney at Fisher Broyles, LLP

Response Sharon Weeks: "Third, the Equal Protection Clause requires states to apply the law equally and prohibits them from discrimination on the basis of race, religion, national origin, or other arbitrary factors. Doesn't say a thing about sex, unless that is an arbitrary factor."

"I was brought up in a matriarchal family where everything was equal and woman assumed to be right. It's taken me a long time to realize and accept that a degree of overcompensation is sometimes necessary to give women the edge on already weighted agendas. I used to think they were strong enough, it's demeaning to give them a head start...my company would have battered me for doing that! However, now that power hungry white males supremacist anthropogenesis have taken the White House I am 100% for...total overcompensation on every front to keep things closer to balance. Especially when the only idiots that will do the dirty work for the president are family!! YUK" **(Andrew McAvoy)** Director at Retool Architecture

"The only comment I can make is: after being a single Mom for years I moved to North Carolina from New York. My saving grace for being a woman, I owned and sold a house in New York. Just to start my utilities in the house I purchased in NC required my SS#...and forget about the mentality when trying to get any sizable project done...they only want to speak to my husband...anyone who says that gets hung up on...I don't work with lower mentalities!! When I was divorced with 2 kids my eyes were opened and I saw a whole discriminatory world I had no idea existed until then!!" **(Barbara Ashley)** Molloy College

"Thank you for this! I have just gone over almost all of what you say here with my 19 year old granddaughter who lives with me. She is taking her first women's studies course in college and has to write interview papers, I, the interviewee of the last one because I was born before 1976, in 1950 to be exact. I marched with my older sister for the ERA, participated in pro-choice rallies, know all about the 60's and lack of birth control, as I got pregnant during those years. Making matters worse, I married that horribly abusive man because I felt I "had to" so I could keep my baby. By 1969 I could get the birth control pill, but by then there were stories of pill related cancers everywhere, scary stories...it scared me for sure, and I was pregnant again within 2 months. Fear mongering, I think, as I look back. I have never met even one women who contracted cancer from BCP's! Abortion was still risky then, and not my choice anyway, the key term here being CHOICE. Thus I learned through my own experience what the meaning of CHOICE really is....and that there are many pro-choice people who are also pro-life. (Maybe the opposing groups should be labeled PRO-CHOICE/ANTI-CHOICE?) I also learned how it felt to live subordinately to a man who wielded his "power" over my life, although I was finally able to flee that marriage. Unlike so many decades of women before me who were so completely trapped, I was able to run to the safety of family at the age of 21 with my now 3 little girls and with the law on my side. Women were trapped with no shelters or safe houses to escape to even well into the 1970's; there was nowhere for a woman to escape a brutal situation unless she was lucky enough to have family to take her and her children in, providing shelter and protection like happened to me. I ended up with 5 children all girls, before I reached the age of 26, and it has been my mission to make sure that they and all my granddaughters (grandsons too, for that matter!) know and remember the important history lesson you put forth to all of us here. THANK YOU THANK YOU, THANK YOU. Well done, Ms. Weeks!" **(Barbara Russell Piotrowski)** WSU

S Weeks Response: "Thank you so very much for your comments!"

"In 1984 in Oklahoma if a woman inherited money half of it became the property of her husband, but if he inherited, it was all his. This was not changed until 1987. I was the very first outside sales woman for the company where I worked, and I forged the way for many other women behind me in that and other companies. Male executives thought that it was their right to demand sexual remuneration for sales and promotions – the young women have no idea what our generation went through so this is important." **(Janet Wood Cunliffe)** CEO at Fashion Fit Formula

"Excellent historical article up to present. As an African American woman I take nothing for granted as my people are still fighting for equality in spite of laws being passed, it is the mind set of people." **(Ajike**

Williams) Pastry Chef Instructor, Cakes Uniquely Yours School

"My greatest fear is the rights that were so hard won even in the span of my lifetime will be eroded. Women of today will not know what they have until they lose their rights. Let's all hope that doesn't happen." **(Cathy Minch)** Converse College

Chapter II

Marches

Civil Rights Marches 1960's

From original article: *Again people were beaten, drowned and hanged. Because of the media, there was more attention and the marches for these rights were better known. After the Civil War the 14ᵗʰ and 15ᵗʰ Amendments adopted in 1868 and 1878 granted citizenship and suffrage to blacks, but not to women. A suffrage amendment to the federal Constitution was presented to Congress and repeatedly failed to pass.*

Since 2017 much has happened. Many people were under the impression that civil rights had progressed much farther than they actually had. The use of video on cell phones was a shocking picture into what was actually happening for those of us who were not suffering from racial discrimination. Seeing one young black man after another being shot in the back made racial discrimination front and center and made it impossible to be unaware any longer. The murder of George Floyd in Minneapolis, MN in 2020, on video, affected people all over the world. Months later riots and protests continue. Shortly thereafter the country mourned the passing of Senator John Lewis, the face of the nation for civil rights.

+

Comments: Printed as received without editing.

A few of the comments on the article addressing racial issues as relating to women's rights:

"Thank you! We have a similar history in the UK and women in Switzerland did not get the vote till the 1960's. It's worth pointing out that while white women endured all this exclusion and violence, it was and is black women who bore the brunt of the institutionalized misogyny. And in huge areas of the world today, women and girls are still beaten, mutilated, sold and trafficked for their gender. Young women in privileged parts of the world (the USA) perhaps have no idea how lucky they are and what struggles have gone on for them to be free. It did not happen by itself." **(Griselda Cann Murssett)** Distributor, Juice Plus+

"I would like to add that during the Suffrage movement, Black women were often excluded, or discouraged from participating. It's important to know the history of racism in the feminist movement, because we need to move past that and work together to insure civil rights for ALL women." **(Leslie Toussaint)** Ellicott City, Maryland

"This may be true for white women, but black women still suffer inequality and when the feminist movement was started it was because white women wanted more power, but it did not include black women...we have supported fought and died for your power...when have you supported ours...the recent marches were hailed as non-violent, but when we march we are a mob. Please, this article is not to empower black women but to empower whites." **(Chery Hicks)** Antioch University , Los Angeles

S Weeks Response: "It shouldn't be that way and unless we are united change isn't going to work."

"Great Summary. One correction: *After the Civil War, the 14th and 15th amendments adopted in 1868 granted citizenship and suffrage to blacks, but not to women. These amendments gave Black men the right to vote. Not Black women. We didn't gain the right to vote until 1920, the same as all women. This is an important fact. Native American women were dealing with their own set of issues as well. When you say women you are often meaning White women. There are nuance and facts that are important to include in these narratives. Particularly around race. Thank you again for taking time to outline this history." **(Niki Bas)**

Other Marches

"I needed this information in this concise form. Some of my friends responded to the women's March with "what do these women want?" Thank you so much for putting my feelings on paper. I can now share!" **(Linda Ellis)**

"We "women" have all come a long way, but apparently, we haven't come far enough. The Women's March was not only about women, but about everyone that needed a voice during these turbulent times. Most of us fear losing these "privileges" we have fought so hard for. We don't want to go back in time. That's why I think this is not just a women's movement, but a progressive movement. I think women marched because we make good protectors of these rights. We marched because we know the struggles of

109

others. We choose to march not only for ourselves, but for others as well. Why? Because it's kind of hard to call in the guard and fire-hose women and children when we protest peacefully. So, while some people want to remind us that we have come a long way (and should be grateful,) I would like to remind them that we wouldn't be marching again if we felt like we were done. We are not of the "privileged" class yet, we have a long way to go and work yet to do." **(Hilary Bilodeau)** Fine Art Teacher at Elementary School

"What have you lost since Jan 20, 2017? No purpose defined except uteruses on your heads. Nobody is for life- that group was forbidden to march. Sorry, your not my march!" **(Kuku Prylinski)** Huntsville, Alabama

"I marched in the D.C. women's march the day after inauguration with my two daughters, 26 & 23 years old. I must say that I have marched before ....40 years ago...and did not think I'd need to do it again? But I realize that if anything will change in America, it will happen because of us women. No one else! A young woman asked me at the march if this day was a deja vu for me. That's when I realized how much there is still to accomplish. Women today need to be vigilant about maintaining the fight for equal rights. Complacency will thrust us backwards." **(Monica Pappas)** Carnegie Mellow University

"My 79 year old mother marched in DC for women's rights, civil rights and again in 1/21/17 at the Women's March in DC, but for this March her granddaughter/we pushed her in a wheelchair. She still has a handful of buttons from a March decades ago that say, "Give Women Credit". For all

110

the women who suffered, marched and demanded equal rights over the last 200 years, this should be a reminder to the young women today whom have become complacent to NEVER take freedom for granted." **(Darby Fertitta Mckaine)** Realtor at Douglas Realty
S Weeks Response: "Thank you and thanks for pushing your mom."

"I totally agree with your article. Well said! Because most of these women have had these rights all along, they take it for granted. It really frightens me when I think how quickly we could lose those rights and refer back to older times. Right now, the White House wants to take us back 100 years if they're able to. We can't take these rights for granted. We need to stay informed, be vigilant, and take a stand by showing our united from against the freedoms the government could take away. Writing Congressmen, Senators, marching for women's rights are some of the things we need to do." **(Angela Green)** Educational Interpreter for the Deaf at Evansville Vanderburgh School Corporation

"While this piece does lay out an informative summary of matters of historical import in our effort to further women's rights, the opinions expressed by the author on her views of "young women" ring untrue and somewhat disrespectful. Please correct me or better inform me from a woman's perspective, but the author's opening statement, written in the context of the Women's March on Washington, "that many young women are completely satisfied with their lives right now", referred to by the author as "status quo", strikes me as patently false. Was participation in the Women's March itself not a clear expression of thorough dissatisfaction with the "status quo", am I missing something here? The young women I attended the march with and those I spoke with and listened to and read the handmade signs of expressed immense dissatisfaction with the "status quo". The author also claims that "you probably didn't know that in the 1870's women could not own property, could not sign contracts, could not vote, file lawsuits, nor have their own money." Again, I must disagree with the author, young women definitely know these things, especially on the issue of a constitutionally guaranteed right to vote. Furthermore, young people also know "that a select group of white men, a board of education in Texas, (being) charged with the job of editing all of the history   textbooks for decades" is a root cause as to why these important women's issues are not covered sufficiently in text books. We do know these things, both the issues themselves and the insufficiency of textbooks, because we have and utilize many different sources of knowledge, including the internet. In the end, I very much agree with the author's healthy reminder to remain vigilant and to not become complacent, however, those who are currently challenging the status quo most aggressively and radically are young women! Reading this piece again, I would love to know who the author has in mind when she says "young women". Her well-intentioned, yet possibly patronizing, commentary seems much better suited if directed toward adolescent girls in the elementary or middle school rather than toward young women in the 20's and 30's who are engaged civically and are actively organizing and participating in mass demonstrations at the Women's March." **(Nick Gauthier)** U Conn

Response S Weeks: "I did clearly state that "some young women" may not know, and made a reference to comments on Facebook that helped make up my mind to write the article. The comments belittled the marchers and referred to them as whiners and also stated they were in complete charge of their lives. Many young women do not know their history. I wanted them to know about marches and how valuable they can be. It wasn't aimed at all women or all young women. It was never meant to be disrespectful. I found the disrespect in comments made about the marchers. I hope this clears it up for you. Many miss the title "What Young Women May Not Know."

"Marched for the woman's right in 1972 on the streets of Paris....shocked to learn that French woman did not have the right to have her own bank account without her husband's signature....that was my first eye opening experience..." **(Sachiko Chiba Reis')**

"Brilliant aid. Would someone please see all marchers get copies when there is another March. I think we are at the beginning of a March era. AGAIN" **(Pamela Webster)** Ely, Minnesota

"Fantastic review of how it was. I, too, urge young women who "don't see what all the marching, protesting and posting is about" to not take it for granted. Right now, the U.S. is at the edge of a dark canyon of rights." **(Twila Sears)** Truman State University

"Thank you for writing this down concisely. At 74, I'm aghast that we're still marching and carrying signs. Let's work together on the streets, in the boardrooms and in our homes to push for equality of opportunity for our daughters and granddaughters and for the men who suffer if women can't contribute their best to the world." **(Orick Peterson)** Freelance writer for OP Communications

"Hurrah for you and the thoughtful comments. During a recent March I carried a sign from the Women's Rights National Historical Park. No one recognized the sign or knew about the Park or Seneca Falls. A bit of history needs to be shared. Thanks for the post." **(Elizabeth Kelly)** Houston, Texas

"Very nice article. In 1952, my mother, who had divorced my father due to his abuse of her, was working for Cities Service (no Citgo) and asked for a raise. Her boss went to bat for her, but was told "If I'm going to pay that much, I'll hire a man," and she lost her job. So I'll add my voice. I'm glad the young women feel safe. I marched for the rights you enjoy. My grandmother was a suffragette. My mother lost a job just for asking for a raise. Pay attention." **(Sandi Hefter Herrmann)** Retired pastor, Wisconsin Conference United Methodist Church

"I tried to explain this to a 40 yr old woman who could just not understand the reason women were marching. "They have full rights and everything they want now." My heart is breaking for these women whose history education was so lacking." **(Kathy Wright Flynn)**

"Awesome read! I'm turning 80 this year and remember many marches of the past! We've come a long way and further to go!!" **(Barb Johnson)** Coon Rapids, Minnesota

"This is what I've been trying to tell people for so long! This is why we cannot just sit and hope it all works out. We have to stand up and march, stand up and make phone calls, send e-mails, go in person and get others involved, too. Don't let anyone send us back to the old days." (**Cathy Wellner**)

"Perhaps I could have been more supportive of the Woman's March if, 1. There wasn't a widely publicized argument between black women and white women that preceded the march. 2. That the Sharia-law supporting Linda Sarsour, a viscous enemy to Aryan Hirsi Ali, and advocate for women's rights in Islam, wasn't using the March for her own barely-hidden aims, that have nothing whatsoever to do with feminism and Western concepts of free speech, due process and liberty. 3. That the neo-feminists (3rd ware) hunkered down in silence during the investigation and trial of Kermit Gosnell, a murdering butcher of live born babies. While out slaying dragons, new wave feminism has become a dragon itself, feeing into the suppression of speech in colleges and on the streets. Clean up your act, Vagina-hat clowns." (**Joyce Clemons**) Cardinton, Ohio

"For those of us who are old enough to either remember or have taken part in the protests of the 1960's and 1970's, most of what is happening today comes flooding back as the horrors of injustice of those earlier times. At that time, I did what I could, even barely into my teens in the 60's to fight against those injustices. Many people seem to laugh in the face of the injustices shown by the new president, his administration, his party and his supporters, thinking that the protestors who take to the streets are foolish and over-

115

reacting. I am here to say that this is not a kneejerk reaction and we who fought for the progress that has been made will fight again. Those wonderful young people who are socially conscious are joining the protests in huge numbers. It warms my heart to see them come out in such huge numbers. Perhaps we can prevent the loss of so many freedoms that were won through so many hard fought efforts. Peace to all of you!" **(Harvey Tanttila)** Sebeka Secondary

"All this is true and disturbing. It wasn't the march It self, it was the vulgarity that was displayed there. Made me ashamed to be female." **(Christine N. Ray Whitt)** Registered Nurse at Appalachian Regional Healthcare **Response from Stacy Marie**: "5 million people marched around the world. 673 marches took place worldwide, on all seven continents, including in 29 in Canada, 20 in Mexico and one in Antarctica and you are ashamed to be female. I dare say, you're in the minority. Vulgarity. That's what you're concerned about – not the reason WHY so many people are marching. Wow!"

"I have read and are aware of the strides women have taken. Why do you know more about how I feel as a woman. I am happy with my life. I do NOT need anyone telling me that I don't understand what's been done for me. Contrary to so many liberal beliefs, I am not stupid! Stop telling me I should be out there marching. What is smart about walking around with a vagina hat on my head or standing stark naked in front of Trump Tower. That certainly is classy and full of self respect." **(Diane Schacht)**

Sharon Weeks: "I did not respond. She apparently read a different article than the one I wrote."

"Thanks. I just joined a Women's Rights group at the General Meeting of the Indivisible Movement hr in Asheville, NC. This Narrative on Marches for Rights is most informative. Thank you." **(Barbara Gravelle)** Wayne State University

"I was one of the first women in Texas history to get a car loan in my name – in 1974! I marched thanks to the aid of my walker January 17 – Women and girls protect your rights or you will lose them!!!!" **(Nancy B. Wiggins)** University of Texas at Arlington

"As a young girl 51+, I and many of my friends marched on the capital. On several occasions: fighting against the Vietnam War, Civil Rights, Women's Rights and injustice. Many of us would chip in for gas, bring brown bag lunches and a sleeping bag. We got tear gassed and many beaten, but we showed up for many of these because our friends and family members being sent to Vietnam. Some coming home & some not...We are now in much more serious times and most people are living in a bubble trying to pretend that we are safe from the evils we conquered in the past; but History does repeat itself. We should take heed to remember this and always Vote & Stand for What You Believe In!" **(Patti Obrien Nixt)**

"I needed this information in this concise form. Some of my friends responded to the women's March with "what do

117

these women want?" Thank you so much for putting my feelings on paper. I can now share!" **(Linda Ellis)**

"I have to ask, with all the people marching and taking "Action," what does it take to get the Government to file another "Equal Rights Amendment" and take another vote?" **(John Gagnon)**

"Sharon, thanks for putting his out there...very important for young women to know and to stir them out of complacency and into action (more mature company as well.) I was sent this by one of my nieces. I will say that I was pleased to see that she & her sister & my daughters & myself (Phoenix) in different parts of the US & abroad all marched. Here in PHX many were young.....all a good sign." **(Linda Cohen)** Ottawa University, Arizona

"Thank you for the second "Wake up Call." The first, for me, was getting up on January 21, 2017 and marching with an unbelievable amount of women in Oakland – a march I had not really thought about until a few days before. Since then, I have re-educated myself on "Rights" we have, are losing, will lose under #45. And yes, the realization that ERA has not yet passed. I'm old enough to have cast my first vote for JFK. I'm healthy enough to fight not to lose ground in these terrible times we live in!" **(Liz DeCarli Baker)**

"As I am a 70 year old woman I have lived what you speak and I have experienced threats and intimidation by men, doctors, police and employers. Prior to being 30 I just accepted "status quo" and was unaware of the systemic

118

problems and ownership and control of myself and all women. Since that time many things have changed for women and I have also seen and feared the seeming complacency of our young women. For this reason I was delighted to see the turnout at these most recent marches in the USA and the world. Like so many other happenings in our world, we must never forget the past. And we need to stand together prepared to fight for our freedom as women and human beings, for our sisters, our daughters and all next generations. It makes my heart proud to see this support. Thank you to all the people, women and men, who took the time and effort to be heard and fight for all our rights and freedom." **(Pat White)** MacEwan University

"This describes why I have marched for the most of my life and I am a great grandmother and still marching, signing petitions, writing to government officials and organizing consciousness raising groups. I hope that this generation is not complacent and not taking everything for granted. March, protest, write to your senators, file petitions and most of all vote like your life is on the brink of disaster because it is." **(Deanna J. Williams)**

"I was reminded by a respected elder woman that women of the 60s/70s had to demonstrate at their college campuses for the right to wear pants. They marched, had sit-ins, fought college boards and administrative leaders (probably white males) all for the right to wear trousers. Let that sink in. If you are a woman who criticizes women for demonstrating, please stop wearing pants." **(Mary Kuentz)** Waimea, Hawaii County, Hawaii

"And what exactly are the rights that YOU personaly don't have. Just tell me one. These women are marching for women's rights, but the rights they want they already have and they don't realize it. For example, the wage difference among women and men. Women claim this is one of their inequalities. Have you read the RECENT literature and research and findings? Do YOU realize that women in the same job, with the SAME education working the SAME hours and doing the exact duties ARE being paid the same as a MAN. You feminist rights women and the damage you're actually doing to young women.... "**(Ginny Johnson Winters)** Great Falls College MSU **S Weeks Response:** "Nowhere did I say that I, or any other women in this country, don't have rights. The whole point of the article was to make women aware of how they came to have those rights and to be aware that they could lose them. Please reread it."

Please refer to Chapter V, page 136, and the article on Women's Admission to Asylums in the United States of America (and the Diagnoisis that put them there)

"I know the history of women in our country and others. I question the timing of the women's march which was really all about not liking Trump. Why were they not marching last year or the year before that or the year before that?" **(Caroline Etty Renick Robinson)** Beitar Illit

"At the Women's March a friend of mine stood on the steps of the Raeburn Building and looked into the eyes of each young woman as she passed and asked, "did you vote?" Almost all of them looked panicked and said, "No, but I will." They better." **(Ann Riordan)** Elmira College, Elmira, NY

"My Grandmother help march and fight for these rights told me when I was just a small child, soon as you get old enough get to the polls and vote. I have not missed a vote since I was 18 years old. For it was a white man's world only. The people of color and women had no say and all were treated like white men's property. So we pushed on and Upward. Never let them push us back. We stand together or we fall. So let's stand, all people of color and all women. We will not let the horrible white men take our rights away." **(Carol Wilder)** Scottsboro, Alabama

"We get it, but what are you marching for NOW? I have never had a problem, based on my gender. In 2017, if you are experiencing some sort of slight, look to something else, other than your gender." **(Roxann Nelson)** East Islip, New York
S Weeks Response: "I think you missed the whole point of the article.

"Thank you for reminding us all that we can only March because others marched before us." **(Ardis Cray)**

"Great Article. I heard a phrase the other day that fits this to a tee. "Today's generation of women who are in their 30's-40's and roll their eyes at the women's marches are too comfortable resting on the laurels of the hard-fought battles of their mothers and grandmothers." I don't think they know how quickly the rights they have taken for granted can so easily be ripped away from them. Your explanation does a great job of explaining just how close to the edge they are." **(Greg Schwanzl)** Tampa Florida

Since the George Floyd murder in Minneapolis, MN this summer Jacob Blake in Kenosha, Wisconsin, was shot seven times in the back in August of this year (2020) marches have taken place all over the world.   The Constitution gives people the right to assemble and that includes peaceful protests.   Unfortunately there are people who gravitate to these marches with the intent to riot, burn, property is stolen and property is destroyed, people are killed.   It is a terrible consequence that doesn't need to happen. **BLACK LIVES MATTER** and after one black man after another is killed in racial violence, the need to protest for change intensifies. The violence is terrible and distracts from the people who want nothing but to change racial injustice.

There have been so many more murders since.

Chapter III

Title IX

From the original article: *1972 Title IX is a landmark federal civil right that prohibits sex discrimination in education. Title IX is not just about sports and it protects all students; the federal government threatened to stop aid to all public schools that did not correct this*

The article stopped there, editing did not allow more information. The details of Title IX follow, and comments follow the detail.

Title IX and Sex Discrimination

U.S. Department of Education
Office for Civil Rights
400 Maryland Avenue, SW
Washington, D.C. 20202-1328
Revised April 2015

Title IX

The U.S. Department of Education's <u>Office for Civil Rights</u> (OCR) enforces, among other statutes, Title IX of the Education Amendments of 1972. Title IX protects people from discrimination based on sex in education programs or activities that receive Federal financial assistance. Title IX states that: No person in the United States shall, on the basis of sex, be excluded from participation in, be denied the benefits of, or be subjected to discrimination under any education program or activity receiving Federal financial assistance.

Scope of Title IX

Title IX applies to institutions that receive federal financial assistance from ED, including state and local educational agencies. These agencies include approximately 16,500 local school districts, 7,000 postsecondary institutions, as well as charter schools, for-profit schools, libraries, and museums. Also included are vocational rehabilitation agencies and education agencies of 50 states, the District of Columbia, and territories and possessions of the United States.

Educational programs and activities that receive ED funds must operate in a nondiscriminatory manner. Some key issue areas in which recipients have Title IX obligations are: recruitment, admissions, and counseling; financial assistance; athletics; sex-based harassment; treatment of pregnant and parenting students; discipline; single-sex education; and employment. Also, a recipient may not retaliate against any person for opposing an unlawful educational practice or policy, or made charges, testified or participated in any complaint action under Title IX. For a recipient to retaliate in any way is considered a violation of Title IX. The ED Title IX regulations (Volume 34, Code of Federal Regulations, Part 106) provide additional information about the forms of discrimination prohibited by Title IX.

OCR's Enforcement of Title IX OCR vigorously enforces Title IX to ensure that institutions that receive federal financial assistance from ED comply with the law. OCR evaluates, investigates, and resolves complaints alleging sex discrimination. OCR also conducts proactive investigations, called compliance reviews, to examine potential systemic violations based on sources of information other than complaints.

In addition to its enforcement activities, OCR provides technical assistance and information and guidance to schools, universities and other agencies to assist them in voluntarily complying with the law. OCR's Title IX Resource Guide PDF (501K) is a useful tool for schools and their Title IX coordinators to understand schools' obligations under Title IX.

For assistance related to Title IX or other civil rights laws, please contact OCR at OCR@ed.gov or 800-421-3481, TDD 800-877-8339.

Comments: Printed as received without editing.

"Until reading Sharon Weeks' essay I had forgotten about the restrictions I faced when purchasing my 1st car, obtaining a credit card in my name only, being asked on a job interview if I had or planned to have children, not going to college because I believed my only options were to be either a teacher of a nurse. My parents encouraged my brother to seek a higher education, but felt my future should be getting married and having children, in other words, to become a "housewife." It was mandatory then in middle school to take Home Economics which consisted in a semester of learning a pittance about cooking and another semester of sewing. The first project was making a gathered skirt which included a zipper or in those days called a placket. I graduated from high school in 1958 so it was not all that long ago. Oh, also, completive sports were not in the curriculum for young women." **(Mary Strickler)**

"This is so true. My hair stylist couldn't believe abortion could be illegal. She has no real understanding of Watergate, the draft or Vietnam. It's sad that when I tell women that they have a moral imperative to vote because of what the women endured to get the vote they look at me like I'm crazy. Likewise, when I'm asked what sport I played in high school I laugh. Women's athletics didn't exist when I was in high school." **(Jeanne Clemens)**

"There were separate job ads and women could only be secretaries or teachers, but had to quit if they were married and pregnant. Title 9 (IX) finally required Harvard to admit women. Supreme Court Justice Sandra Day O'Connor, who was second in her law school class couldn't get hired as a lawyer, only as a legal secretary, since she was a woman. Health care plans have been able to limit what health care women receive since "men were treated equally" since they didn't get maternity or contraception birth control coverage either." **(Maura Garcia)** Bryn Mawr College

Friday, November 30, 2018 DEVOS' **TITLE IX CHANGES OPEN FOR PUBLIC COMMENT** Seattle Times   Education Secretary Betsy DeVos has proposed narrowing schools' obligations when it comes to responding to sexual misconduct. Public comment has opened, and people may now tell the U.S. Department of Education what they think about her desired changes to Title IX regulations. DeVos' proposal is a departure from President Barack Obama era guidance for Title IX, a federal civil rights law that prohibits gender discrimination in schools that receive public funding. These changes, DeVos has said, would make the process fairer to accused students and their schools.

The proposal – leaked in September and officially released by the Education Department mostly unchanged this month-has been denounced by survivors and their advocates, who believe it will allow schools to avoid dealing with cases of sexual misconduct.

Public comment opened Thursday and lasts for 60 days – meaning people have until about the end of January to share their thoughts.

What changes? Schools would only be required to respond if an official report was made to them or if multiple complaints about the same person were made to an official with authority to respond. (Under Obama, schools could be found in violation of their Title IX obligations for not responding to sexual misconduct if they knew or reasonably should have known about it.)

Schools also wouldn't have to respond to off-campus incidents, and the definition of sexual harassment would be narrower.

Other controversial changes include allowing schools to use a higher standard of evidence and mediation for sexual-misconduct cases, as well as requiring cross-examination by advisers during hearings.

Jess Davidson, executive director of End Rape on Campus, said she and other advocates have been working to improve the Title IX process for survivors and that DeVos' changes would roll back that progress.

Times News Service

Chapter IV

Roe v Wade

From 2017 Article: 1973 Roe v Wade *made abortion legal and safe. Women stopped dying from abortions. The government is planning to stop funding for Planned Parenthood and tens of thousands of women will not only lose coverage for basic health care, but they will also no longer have access to birth control. That pretty much means there will be more unwanted pregnancies and if Roe V Wade is overturned, which seems likely with the appointment of a new Supreme Court judge by this administration, there will be more women dying from abortions again.*

This section of the article received many, many comments. There were too many to include all of them but I have tried to gather a fair cross-section. They follow:

Comments: Printed as received without editing.

"I part ways with the current Women's movement when it comes to the life of the unborn. With all do respect, I cannot understand how Women's Rights means pro-abortion, and how the direction changed. What I know of history, and from what I've read, these great women sufferagettes were against abortion, but were adamantly for equal rights. Elizabeth Cady Stanton, Sara F. Norton, Victoria Woodhull, Maddison Brinckerhoff, Dr. Elizabeth Blackwell, Susan B.

Anthony, Dr. Charlotte Lozier and more." **(Renee Hanks)** Office Manager at Redding Stem Academy

"Unbelievable that she references Margret Sanger, an open racist who did more to oppress Black Americans in the 20th century than any other single person. The problems faced by women today would virtually all disappear if men, worldwide, would treat them with the respect and honor that is their God-given right. If human beings would live like humans, not animals, abortion as a form of birth-control would be unnecessary". **(Thomas Nunamaker)** Property Accountant, Fieldwood energy LC

S Weeks Response: "Margaret Sanger was a part of history."

"**1973: Roe v Wade** hizo aborto legal y seguro. Las mujeres dejaron de morir a causa de abortos....O SEA QUE HACE CUATRO DIAS TODAVIA MORIAMOS COMO MOSCAS DESANGRADAS EN MESAS DE CARNICEROS. **(Isabel Steva Hernandez)**" Sagrado Corazon, Santruce, Puerto Rico

S Weeks Response: I am apologizing in advance for any inaccuracies made in this translation. "1973: Roe v Wade made abortion legal and safe. Women stopped dying from abortions....OR IS THAT FOUR DAYS AGO WE STILL DIED LIKE BLOODY FLIES ON BUTCHERS TABLES." (Isabel Steve Hernandez) Sagrado Corazon, Santruce, Puerto Rico

"Excellent piece of history! I do not agree with spreading fear and rumors about rights and abortion being reversed, however. Plus, the government and tax payers don't need to

FUND abortion and birth control. Both are available. (**Lisa Partridge Ramsbottom**) "Real Estate Broker, Keller William Realty

S Weeks Response: "The government does not fund abortions. And birth control is not always available for the young victims of incest."

"If planned parenthood wasn't selling baby parts and human tissue I have no objection. This BS that they'll loose basic healthcare is just that B. I have no issue with abortion on grounds of rape or incest. But for my tax dollars going just because they couldn't keep their legs closed is BS. Time women take responsibility for their actions. There's the morning after pills and such." (**Frederick Kithcard**)

Sharon Weeks: "I should have answered this one, but sometimes you just know some people won't accept facts, etc."

"Why do women's rights always come down to abortions? This entire article couches in hyperbole and fear and it is all about abortion. No, women aren't going to go backwards. Unless we get Sharia law from the Muslim high birth rate taking over. So I'd say, have babies, lots of them, if you don't want women's rights to go backwards." (**Wendy Cole**)

S Weeks Response: "This was most certainly not all about abortion."

"While this impassioned speech is wonderful and true to a point, it contains a red herring, which the author may not have intentionally included, as her opinions run evenly with that opinion. However, it is my opinion, that the freedom to live openly as a same sex couple, does negate in any way

130

with my freedom to open a bank account as a woman. I am not insisting on adding at third gender. Hence, the red herring. Also, inserted, as a red herring, was the view that if we lose the right to government (public, or in other words, tax money) money for abortion clinics, we are somehow being forced to return to a time I grew up in, the 1960's, and that would be bad. I was one of those women who had sex before marriage, and being responsible for myself, I said to my boyfriend, well, we could get married and we did. We did not have a pretty wedding, or a college education, then, anyway, but we did have a son who grew up to be a software Engineer for Intel. And has patent filed in his name. He is a strong Christian leader and a great husband and father. And he would just be dead if he was one of those abortions you people advocate. The best and most wonderful job a woman can have, in addition to all the others we are offered, is being someone's Mom. I loved it." **(Jean Teague)** Big Spring High School

S Weeks Response: "Thanks for your comments. The marches were listed to show the women who criticized the marchers as whiners that marching has taken place for many causes and aided those causes, too."

"Astounded that, after all these years, so many fail to grasp that the abortion issue is yet another money issue. It's not about "life." Rather it's about preventing middle and low-income women the right to control their own body. Historically the wealthy have always had access to a safe medical procedure – even when abortion was illegal. Abortion will never go away and it is NO ONE's business but that of the woman who chooses to have one." **(Pamela Grow)** Founder at Basics & More Fundraising

"I've always said to myself, "think like a man" when interviewing for a job and asking for equitable wages. But when it comes to being a mother, and protecting children, I am a Mother Bear. Don't fuck with me. That said, I'm pro choice because I believe the women who had abortions made the right choice at the time they could not support a child and could not witness the poverty and struggle of survival raising a child without food or shelter. Yes, 1 in 4 children in the US live in poverty, and with the current president it will get worse. Those white male politicians need to lose health insurance, food on the table and be homeless for awhile, before they dictate how we women should live!" **(Melanie Moynan-Smith)** Ohio University **S Weeks Response**: "I think they either need to have the health insurance the rest of us have or they need to make sure we have the health insurance they have!"

"So easy to take for granted those freedoms. So easy to lose them. I'm close to 70 and clearly remember the fear of an unwanted pregnancy. Too many women endured ugly, painful deaths when they had to resort to back alley abortion. We MUST remain alert, and we MUST educate those fortunate women and girls who do not know the terror of women who came before them." **(Cyndy Renoff)** Baltimore, MD

"I agree with "almost" all of this, with the exception of Margaret Sanger, or at least her motives. She was a prejudiced bigot. She wanted minority women to have abortions to control minority population. Look it up. I have no respect for her, regardless of abortion rights for all. **(Kim**

132

Bergsma) Grand Rapids Christian High School **S Weeks Response:** "There are many differing articles on Margaret Sanger, but I chose to include her as she was a part of history."

"1973 Roe v Wade made abortion legal and safe. Women stopped dying from abortions." Wrong. No medical procedure is without risk. **"(Betsy Jeffries Springer) S Weeks Response:** "There is a definite difference in the risk, though, between a back-alley abortion and a procedure done in a hospital."

"Thank you for this condensed version. I'm old enough to know about this history and have lived through some of it, but you are right, many young women do not know our history. During the Women's march in Seattle, a young women asked me what Roe v Wade meant which I had printed on the poster that I made to carry in the march. I was glad that she asked and happy to explain but sorry that she did not know." **(Barbar Bader)**

"I remember being quite young – 12 or 13 – when my Mother revealed to me that she'd had to go to Mexico to get an abortion in the 50's. It was a "back-room" abortion in a dentist's office (she was unmarried, a starving artist with no means to support a child.) She almost bled to death, and had blood poisoning afterwards. She was so ill she couldn't drive or fly home to NYC and had to remain in Mexico for months, relying on the kindness of strangers to eat. I will NEVER forget WHY we must fight for Roe v Wade. Women died. And PLEASE don't start about the sanctity of Life when you're unwilling to fund Meals on Wheels, or

allow refugee children and women into OUR country."
(Kate Lanier) Vassar College

"I am very blessed and know that women of the past had a huge struggle to get where we are today. I only disagree with what I see as fear mongering over planned parenthood. I have no issue with birth control, and even as a youngster, I easily paid for my own with no insurance, and no help from pp. Even though I find abortion as America's hilicost, with 58 million abortions since 1973. I do not deny any woman's right to seek this option, but as a pro life woman, I do not feel that my tax dollars should go to fund this option. And my big question is why doesn't pp not give women other options, why no prenatal care? Why not truly offer women's health, not just a killing industry. What is wrong with teaching these girls that if you don't want to get pregnant don't have unprotected sex. There is a consequence, not only the death of an unwanted child, but the emotional detestation these women are left to deal with for the rest of their lives, in addition to risking their own lives just going through this procedure. I'm not trying to discount women's American rights, I just want for other options to be equally offered.." **(Heather Sweitzer)** Kent, Ohio **S Weeks Response:** "I think PP offers many of the things you referred to re health care. Not having sex is just fine, but hard to avoid when being raped or the object of incest."

"I have read a lot of the responses and have to say that those of you who think PP is strictly abortions you are ever so wrong. First no abortions are ever done on tax payer money. Second, the service they offer were a God send to many of us. When I graduated from college and was no longer on my parents insurance I need help due to terrible periods which came sporadically. With very little money and no insurance PP helped me regulate and made my life so much better. There are many that go to them for much needed help." **(Jane Larson Belling)** Carroll University

"That's very interesting the one thing I do not agree with this plan parenthood if you women all women want to have abortions you should all pay for it yourselves not the government. They will never overtime abortions so it will always be legal anybody that wants one should pay for it themselves. Because in the end everybody has to answer to God." **(Ed Mc Donough)** Mount Laurel, New Jersey
S Weeks Response: Government money is not used for abortions.

"I'm going to comment and probably be bashed for it, but I think this is very informative, BUT I do want to say the PP is not what it was originally planned to be. It is out of hand. If they should decide to fund it, it should birth tight controls. When it originated, it was to help the mother make an educated choice, abortion, adoption or to keep the babies. It was also interested in birth control. I have read many, many people's stories about when they went to PP the only choice they were given was abortion. Get back to the original meaning of PP." **(Jo Mcgowan)** Methodist College of Nursing
S Weeks Response: "First thing is that the government does not pay for abortions. And as far as I know, at least in this area, many women go just for the birth control pills."

"It's not only white Christian men who are saying Make American Great Again. Over 60 million people voted for
135

Trump. They were not all WCM. This article is great except for the "right to abortion."Women will NOT lose coverage for basic health care. There are many other places to get that but this will still be available at PP. After all they say only 3% of their business is abortion. It can certainly be funded by private donations .They will also have access to birth control. Can you imagine a world where men are held accountable for having sex? That pretty much means there will be less unwanted pregnancies and if R v W is overturned, which seems likely with the appointment of a new Supreme Court judge by this administration. As for the comment "There will be many more women dying from abortions again." Half the babies aborted are WOMEN. And there are many women who die from legal abortions and the suffer psychological and emotionally as well." **(Judy Folster)**

"In response to another posting: It's called the "morning after pill." If you are raped, call 911, get to a hospital. You will get a pill that prevents a rape pregnancy." (**Sherry Murry**)

"In response to a post by Judy Folster: No, those women WILL be without healthcare. When they say "Defund PP" they mean Defund PP. Federal tax money already cannot be used for abortion. They want to stop reimbursement for birth control, cancer screenings, STI testing, etc. So those women (and men) who live in an area where Planned Parenthood is their ONLY community health option...those people will be without affordable healthcare. Do you really think all those services should have to be paid for by private donation?" **(Jessica Lambert)** Inter. Order of Rainbow Girls

"Responding to a comment that says there are thousands of hospital based women's health clinics, etc. You're kidding right? You think health departments are everywhere? I've never even seen one, but have used PP as my primary care since I was a teen in the '60's. Available, inexpensive, compassionate and professional. It was the ONLY place I could get the pill as an unmarried woman for my HEALTH issues in those days. Thank you PP." **(Lahna Bindrich Young)** UW Madison

"In response to another writer, Dawn Aichele, no matter how much fact is provided, you continue to believe the lies. Fact 1, no tax dollars go toward abortion. Fact 2. PP provides a much needed service in Healthcare to many women who need it. If you are going to provide alternative facts please back it up with examples. For example, what other health facilities provide health care services to women as is provided by PP, and before you rant about abortion I am asking about Healthcare as provided by PP." **(Winne Riddel Sipprell)** Minnetonka, Minnesota

"Don't you know that "birth control" is not the pill? It is abortion. Not moral? Huh? Also five justices gave us Roe. By the way, Roe has disowned her abortion stance. Margaret Sanger was a person who wanted to abort black babies. Genocidal. This woman is a democrat liberal!" **(Gayle Kirkman)** Retired teacher

"My great grandmother was one of those women who lost her life due to an abortion in the early 1900's. I heard stories that my great grandfather was a drinker and was mean when drinking. She had two children and could not bear to have another child at that time. She lost her life. Both her children grew up living in other people's homes and later farmed out to work. It is so important for us all to pay very close attention to what is happening in our country today. We all need to speak up and speak out to educate and fight for our rights that have been gained and to better our world. We do not want to lose those rights and go back in time to those good ole days. It was not so good for many. We need to thank those who gave so much for us to have the rights we do have. There is also so much more that can be done." **(Sherry Lee Meallue Parker)** Embrace, Oregon

"My Mother marched for civil rights and helped arrange "safe" abortions for religious dignitaries when abortion was illegal. This will happen again, the rich and privelged will be able to have safe abortions and the rest will suffer and, yes, many will die." **(Julie Reynolds Reinhart)** Account Executive at Zayo Group

"1973 Roe v Wade. We won't go back!" **(Karen Reilly)** Medina, Ohio

"....women stopped dying from abortions..." No, the didn't. Frequency has decreased, but it still happens. Woemn will "lose...basic health care...."and "lose acess to birth control..." No, they won't, neither of those has EVER been restricted to a single avenue of access. When you overstate your case, you harm it rather than help it. And touting a

138

known eugenicist like Sanger as a heroine doesn't help either." **(Kerry Miller)** Retired

"We must always remember that abortion is not birth control." **(Darlene Baird)** Asst. Music Teacher/American Community School of Abu Dhabi

"Because I note the comments sections drifting over to abortion, it is important to note that R v W has nothing to do with the ERA as R v W was decided on the right to privacy, not a non-existent equal right amendment. As Yale law Journal stated, pregnancy is a unique issue for women and thus is not a question of equal treatment (this is lawyer speak for the obvious, men can't get pregnant.) People who want to withhold equality for women, will try to overlap the issues in an attempt to tie an issue (gender equality) which enjoys a 95% approval rating to an issue far more divisive. R v W. Don't fall for it. The ERA is an equality under law, equality of opportunity, and equality of pay issue, don't allow this important economic issue to be high-jacked in a lazy attempt to divert attention to a more divisive subject. R v W is also important, but in a very different issue realm! In fact, if you want to draw a correlation between the ERA and abortion, as a medical professional, I would say a ratified federal ERA would reduce rates of abortion, why? Because for 4 decades every time I have ever told a woman, you don't have the flu, you're pregnant, if that's not good news the first response is some version of "I can't afford to be pregnant or I can't lose my job." This anecdotal info is backed up by decades of data that show the biggest driver of terminating an unplanned pregnancy is economic stability and upward mobility of all women pregnant or not would reduce abortions that and access to reliable, affordable birth control. Learn more at Women-Matter.org." **(Eileen Davis)** Cofounder at Women-Matter.org

"No sex until you can afford it that's what the nuns taught us. Why should we pay because you were stupid"''
(Pat Moskowitz)
S Weeks Response: "Apparently you have never heard of rape or incest."

"Women are still dying from abortions. So are the babies. The pill can be bought very easy and is cheap. Your own Dr. can put an IUD in. Don't use abortion for birth control".
(Sharon Klippert Thomas)
S Weeks Response: "I would hope that no women use abortion for birth control, but don't forget about the pregnancies caused by rape and incest"

"I can appreciate all of the women's history, and have fought my way out of a father and a husband who tried to dominate and control me in my life. As a property owner and college professor, I am proud of where I am, and don't let myself be bullied by men. However, there is one point I have trouble with. Why do women have sex if they aren't prepared to have a baby? Why is the birth control burden placed on the woman? Men can buy condoms at any drugstore. Women, what are you afraid of? Just say no!! We still have a long way to go. Many women are STILL allowing men to make decisions that they should be making for themselves." **(Kathryn Marie)** University of Louisville
 S Weeks Response: "I don't think "just say no" works with rapists. Not with incest either."

140

"Couldn't agree more with the concept of equality! But I would caution against the elevation of Margaret Sanger. She was a racist who advocated the practice of eugenics...a horrible individual. **(Mike Sleutz)** Chief Operations Officer at GentleBrook

S Weeks Response: "I will state once again that I was not elevating Margaret Sanger. She was a point in history. Since then I have been given a link that corrects some information about her."
https://en.wikipedia.org/wiki/Margaret_Sanger

"Just a quick Question to S Weeks do you believe that most of these subjugations of women was religious based or male based. I am only asking because the Old Testament the original one and Sharia law makes mention of these and enforced them. I am the father of 2 daughters and many granddaughters and nieces and cousins that are female and many do not share your view going forward from the 1970s. I do not know why you entered Sanger in the conversation as she was against black women having babies and maybe some others also her quotes are out there. I believe there is still discrimination to a certain extent out there against women by both women and men but that is a work in progress trying to fix it. Many of the things you cited are without a doubt true but I sense a little political motivation in some of them and this is sad. Fight for women's rights period not some political ideology left or right leaning." **(Ted Harvey Stocking)** Stocker at Menards

S Weeks Response: "Thanks for your comment. I don't know if the subjugations were religious based or male based, probably a combination of the two. Here is a very good

141

article about Margaret Sanger. I put her into the article as she is a part of history. Here is a link https://en.wikipedia.org/wiki/Margeret_Sanger. There was no political motivation at all. Sorry that you thought that. The fight for women's rights is a fight for all people."

"Margaret Sanger is a hero for all women. She worked in poor areas of the NYC where women were overwhelmed with having so many kids they did not want nor could not take care of. There certainly appreciated getting birth control, thanks to her efforts. My own mother, who had seven children, was thrilled to get birth control pill in 1960. She and my father did not want any more children (really, they already had too many.) Margaret Sanger is a hero for all women (except those of you who apparently think all women should spend their lives barefoot and pregnant!)" **(Carol Carpenter)** Retired

"I removed my comments about abortion because they were of my own opinion derived from years of experiences with people who expressed their remorse on the subject. Abortion can be haunting, and that is where my passion came from."
(Denise Nave) Registered Nurse at HealthPoint

"We must not forget nor become complacent, it is amazing that women themselves are not in agreement about these basic rights." **Davi Martin)** Tupperwear

"Birth control should be the pill or get your tubes tied NOT abortion!! Women have the same rights as a man now days you are only marching because trump is defunding plan parenthood don't be a fool ladies unless you like to murder

142

innocent babies you sick twisted people keep your legs closed if you don't want a baby." **(Mandy Bell)**
 S **Weeks Response:** "Have you ever heard of rape or incest?"

November 1, 2020   Amy Coney Barrett was confirmed to the Supreme Court this last week in a previously unheard of rush by the Republican party. She has made her opinion on abortion very clear in the past. We will now see if Roe v Wade stands the test of time, or as many have predicted, we will see the end. As someone else previously said, "It will start with one right, that will just be the beginning."

Sharon Weeks

Chapter V

Women's Health

Things have changed so much in women's health over the years. I think it is important to know just how recent some of these changes that affected women so much are mentioned here. Involuntary sterilization is a subject I knew very, very little about. My research on that awful subject is at the end of this chapter and includes genital mutilation.

Comments: Printed as received without editing.

"In 1964 I needed surgery to remove and test a lump from my breast. It couldn't be done without my husband's permission. He said no! He didn't want a "maimed wife." I have a different husband now." **(Andrea Hill Shelley)**

"So little mention is EVER made of all the women in the 1600's, 1700's, 1800's with high IQ's who wound up committing suicide because they were so belittled and not allowed to use their minds. It's time to shout all this abuse from the housetops. And it's time for all of us to become the storm that blows away this horror." **(Tsandi Crew)** All Over Creation

S Weeks Response: Because of Ms. Crew's comments, I am inserting an article and chart that directly relates to her comments. This article makes references to other pages that

I have not included. You may follow those by going on line to the original article. <u>Lunacy in the 19th Century</u>

Oshkosh Scholar, Page 9<u>, Lunacy in the 19th Century: Women's Admission to Asylums in United States of America</u> Katherine Pouba and Ashley Tianen, co-authors Dr. Susan McFadden, Psychology, faculty adviser

Introduction

Women faced many instances when their normal bodily functions, actions or interests as a woman were considered abnormal or a symptom of insanity. Between the years of 1850-1900, women were placed in mental institutions for behaving in ways male society did not agree. Elizabeth Packard was one of these women. (Packard will be discussed later in more depth.) Women during this time period had minimal rights, even concerning their own mental health. Examples are the status of women concerning their roles in marriage and employment. Women's roles in these areas were minimal and concrete, leading to a second-rate position in society compared to men. "It must be admitted then, that there are causes acting unfavorably upon the chances of insanity among women, the existence of which may be said to be native to the sex" (Tuke, 1864, p. 149). Considered less important than men, women had few rights. Important life decisions including admittance to an asylum were decided by a husband, brother, or male friend. Occasionally, men's societal expectations of how women should act did not coincide with how some women acted. The symptoms qualifying a woman's need for admittance during these times would be considered controversial in the present day. Symptoms such as depression after the death of

145

loved one, use of abusive language, and suppressed menstruation, meaning the lack of menstrual cycle, would not be accepted as reasons for admittance to a mental institution today. Not only were the symptoms controversial according to today's practices, but the diagnoses resulting from the symptoms were also only during this time period. Diagnoses such as epilepsy and nymphomania were not looked at as diseases, but as bouts of insanity. Women were also diagnosed with insanity when they exhibited symptoms of overexertion. The female patients understood as being tired and not insane, considering the expected duties of women and the daily struggles of the 19th century. Further discussions will examine interactions between the role of women, societal expectations, and mental institution commitments. The source of data was found in the admission files and records of patients admitted to Mendota Mental Asylum during the years of 1860-1900. We studied a total of 60 random women who were admitted to this asylum during this time period. This paper will cite 26 of these case studies who fit criteria of being admitted by their husbands or a male. See Table 1 for more in-depth information on the patients discussed throughout this paper. Mendota Mental Asylum has since changed its name to Mendota Mental Health Institute and is located in Madison, Wisconsin. We begin our discussion of women's rights and roles during the 19th century. We refer briefly to Elizabeth Packard, who fought for women's rights during the admission process. Next we discuss and explain the symptoms and diagnoses of the women we studied who were admitted to the Mendota Mental Asylum. Lunacy in the 19th Century 15 Table 1 Information About Women Admitted to Mendota Mental Asylum Between 1869-1872 Table 1 Oshkosh Scholar Page

97 Women in the 19th Century Women's Rights and Roles
During the years between 1850 and 1900, women often held
dismal positions.

Information About Women Admitted to Mendota Mental Asylum Between 1869-1872				
Patient No Children	Age	Ethnicity Diagnosis	Marital	Status
1000	17	Bohemian	Unknown	None
Insane by suppressed menses				
1001	50	German	Single	None
Insane by religious matters				
1011	39	American	Married	Eight
Insane by religious fantasy				
1012	47	German	Married	Eleven
Insane by domestic troubles				
1016	25	Irish	Single	None
Insane by unknown cause				
1350	33	Unknown	Widow	Two
Insane by heredity				
1351	25	Unknown	Married	Two
Insane by overexertion				
1353	59	Unknown	Married	One
Insane by religious matters				
1364	46	Unknown	Married	Eleven
Insane by suppressed menses				
1433	30	Irish	Married	Five
Insane by abortion				
1557	40	Irish	Married	Ten
Insane by loss of property				
877	30	American	Unknown	None
Insane by mental excitement				
2121	57	English	Married	Eight
Insane by overwork and domestic trouble				

Patient No	Age	Ethnicity	Marital	Status
		Children		Diagnosis
2213	50	Unknown	Married	Unknown
Insane by religious excitement				
2234	40	Prussian	Married	Six
Insane by unknown causes				
2268	22	American	Married	One
Insane by childbirth				
2285	N.A.	American	Single	None
Insane by nymphomania				

"I remember when women couldn't get credit in their own right or own property. Men could put their wife, sister or mother, in a mental institution forever or until they saw fit to take them out. Admissions were for the smallest points....like being lazy or hard to be around. Women are still oppressed in The USA" (**Carol Waldo**) St. Paul High School

"Thank you so much. We need more of our foremothers telling us stories. I have my mother's stories from the 1940's through the 60's, 70's, 80's and 90's. the way some women were treated when giving birth...hands tied to steel balls secured to the table and with legs tied spread apart. Given shock treatment for depression (when depression was caused by husband cheating on her while she had 4 babies and gambling his paychecks away.) The stories go on and on and on like this. Women were subjected to the worst kinds of domestic abuse and forced to live in those conditions for a multitude of reasons. We need to make sure

148

our histories are told, so that white men in power do not erase us." **(Iana Quesnell)**

"I was 30 in 1965, had 4 Rh children and had to get my husband's signature on a letter to the hospital board before I could have my tubes tied." **(Lois MacKenzie Boarden)** Asbury Park Schools

"In order to get my tubes tied after my 3rd pregnancy I was told I needed to submit a letter requesting this with the reasons for the request to a hospital review board. My husband needed to submit a letter explaining he was in approval of my request and both letters had to be signed before a notary with notary's seal on each, then sent for review and decision. The process was unable to be completed prior to my delivery. After our daughter's birth my husband's urologist scheduled a time for his vasectomy without any need for approval by me or anyone else. This was in 1975." **(Pamela Crouch Redmon)**

"It was in the 1960's when the "Pill" was legalized, but only for married women. When I went to a doctor in 1967 to get a prescription for birth control pills, I was told that I had to be married. I lied and said that I was engaged and would be getting married in two weeks. I got my pills." **(Renee Bridggs)**

"1960's Could be turned down for a job because you were newly married and might get pregnant. Asked in job interviews about your methods of birth control. If you said you didn't want children, then you were looked upon as being flawed as a woman. If you were working, you endured rampant sexual harassment whether you were married or not. If you got pregnant, you were often fired as soon as they found out. 1972 in PA the credit rating went to the husband even if the wife supported the family. Divorced women could then not get loans without a cosigner. Discrimination against divorced women existed in terms of jobs and even in applying for a store or other credit cards. **(Marilyn J. Tkachuk)** Gilman High School

"My mother dared to speak to her medical doctor about getting a tubal ligation in 1962. .... and was scolded for even considering it without asking permission from her husband first. The doctor said, "I'll give Wally a call myself and we'll decide if it's okay." **(Linda Jorenson)**

"Please protect women's rights. As long as men have access to Viagra, women should have a right to contraception." **(Diane Weeks)** Rock Valley College

"As to birth control, it took so long before our insurance would cover the cost of it, but when the little blue pill came out for men there was little blocking it." **(Linda Callaghan)**

"When I wanted a prescription for the pill in 1965 my doctor wanted to know if it was okay with my husband." **(Susan Buchert)** Platteville, WI

"And remember that in the U.S., women still have very limited access to paid maternity leave." **(Leslie Gaudette)** Langley, British Columbia

"In 1972 I could not have a tubal ligation without written consent from my husband. In 1986 I could only purchase a house on my own if I was single. Once married, credit approval depended on my husband's credit and the house had to be in his name. 1981-1984 I was denied employer contributions to a pension plan and was told I didn't need it because I was "young and pretty and someone would marry me and take care of me." We may have come a long way, but not far enough!" (**Mary Anne Evans-Justin**) Works at Presbyterian Church

"Those women who voted for Mr. Trump have started a movement of their own which could undo many of the gains women have achieved in the last 100 years. It is sad to think that so many young girls may have to refight those battles again in the future if the Republicans have their way! Women need equality with men and definitely should have choices when it comes to controlling what happens with the health of their bodies." (**Robert Tuttle**) Burnt Hills – Baliston Lake Senior High

"1939 my mother had to quit teaching when she married. In 1985, I had to have my husband's permission to get my tubes tied because he might want me to have more children. We had two. I gave him the choice of signing for the tubal or signing divorce papers. He signed." (**Ann Fischer Clifford**)

"1972, Binghamton NY, my new dentist refused to treat me because they did not have my husband's signature affirming that he would be responsible for my debts. I explained that my husband was a student at SUNY and I was the family breadwinner, but no go. He either signed the paper or no treatment for me. Left and tried another dentist – same scenario." (**Karen Hewitt**) San Jose, California

"When I first worked as an operating room nurse in 1963, a woman could not sign her own consent for surgery if she was married. Her husband had to sign the consent!" (**Jane Govatos**) University of Deleware

"I was denied a promotion because I was going to be taking maternity leave when I worked at the Minneapolis Fed in 1983. A few years later, when working for a holding XXX company at a community bank in Minnesota, women were being told they did not qualify for disability following child birth because it was a "self-inflected" disability. (**Mary Leizinger**)

"I remember all the girls who got pregnant and then disappeared during HS. I graduated in 1970. Some would come back with a baby, but most would come back alone. No one talked about what happened to them, where they went. I wonder how they dealt with it." (**Rua Swuft**) Conscious Creative Medicine at Swift Healing

"Not just women. In clinical trials they only use male rats to do testing on which does not take into account the affect of female genetics. This means the drugs created are only effective on half the population. Hopefully it has a positive effect on the other half. Well that's the assumption anyway." (**Rick Ching**) Royal Contracting Co.

"Our rights are hanging by a thread. Haters have made "feminism" a nasty word. It is just another manipulation to keep women in men's control. The majority of the world's women do not have the civil liberties we enjoy today in America. They suffer abuse, rape, female circumcision, lack of work (much less equal pay,) burkas, chaperions to leave their home, they can't work, they can't drive. We have to stand together to keep what we have struggled to gain and pull up the millions of women that are not even there yet. Surprisingly the USA is one of only four countries of the 196 in the world that does not mandate paid maternity leave. I know all of this to be true because I have lived in other countries. I have experienced it for myself. It is heartbreaking. We mustn't slip back, we must stand our ground." **(Lori Sherzer Snow)** Director of Cash Management at Standford University

"In 1973 I went to the only doctor in my small college town to get birth control pills. He refused and gave me a lecture on wanton behavior, even though the pill was legal and I have seldom behaved wantonly. I was so humiliated I left in tears. Young women: believe these things and stand up for your rights!" **(Mary Rohrback)** Mansfield University

"I didn't know my dad's mother, Mildred McMahan Henderson. When my dad was 16 yrs. Mildred was pregnant with the second child. The doctor told her that either she or the baby would live because she was over 40 yrs. (am almost 65 yrs.) I am sure it was a painful decision for her, but she had a backroom abortion and hemorrhaged to death. My dad told me this while we were out for a walk about two years before he passed on. I have a lovely picture of my beautiful grandmother Mildred with my dad. It is so sad. The first Women's March in DC maybe 10 years ago,

153

there was some kind of a women's even in St. Louis, and so I carried a sign "I march for Mildred." The other side: I march for Cindy, a sister-in-law who took her life, as it came out much later in life in therapy that she was raped for years by her grandfather...a big secret. There are so many skeletons in the closets of most families, secrets/lies." **(Jo Thompson)** Prescott College

"Roe v Wade did more than make abortion legal; it made health care accessible. In 1971, as a single woman, I had an ectopic pregnancy. The ONLY reason my health insurance covered the emergency surgery was because it was misdiagnosed as a ruptured appendix. Had it been correctly diagnosed, my insurance would not have paid a penny – since 'maternity benefits" were ONLY available to married women." **(Sara Jenkins)** Communications Director at Sisters of St. Joseph of Concordia

"Growing up I was aware that most families were large. My grandmother had 18 pregnancies. Only 12 survived. I thought this was done to provide more hands to work the farm land. Actually, it was because there was no safe form of birth control. My Mother had five pregnancies. Only one survived, me. Even if birth control had been available, most families were too poor to afford it. Some say Planned Parenthood (Pp) subsidizes abortions. Those who oppose that Pp provides contraceptives probably have never had a child they could not feed or provide healthcare for a sick baby. I oppose abortions, but I fully understand the need to have Pp funded and staffed with certified personnel." **(Patricia Lee)** University of Akron

"I know many of my friends think I am overzealous with my liberal views. I admit, I am just that. This is just one of the things that have shaped my view. The destruction part now in power is attempting to destroy women's rights as well as most other social reforms that have been fought for and won over the years. Health care, veterans care, education, care of the environment, workers rights, as well as many other issues are on the chopping block. If people sit back and think that it doesn't matter to you who is elected, these things will happen because the destruction part will win". **(Gary Swart)** University of Washington (also printed in an earlier chapter, fits in both)

"Women who want abortion will get one – or die trying. It was illegal in 1969. I was 18 and had just started college. My mother made all the arrangements. We flew to Puerto Rico and stayed at the Hilton and had room service. It was cushy. The Women's Hospital in Santurce was our destination. I was lucky; my family had money and my mother was incredibly brave and she managed to keep it a secret from the rest of our family. Yes, I marched for Roe v Wade. And it grieves me that in 2017 this very private matter is made the business of complete strangers who want to decide how my life (or your life) should be. I was safe because we were monied. Many others were not. To this day, I don't know if my other sisters now. I kept this a secret until just recently – abortion is such a lightening rod subject. But these stories need to be told. You don't want to go back to the not too distant past when women were at risk just for being women. I fear for those who don't have

access to safe healthcare due to lack of financial resources."
(Nina Buckler Eckhoff) University of New Hampshire

"When I was four years old, a playmate of mine was seriously injured while we were playing. Our mothers rushed her to the emergency room while we prayed she did not bleed out before we arrived. This was 1967 and the hospital refused to treat her because her father was not present to give permission for treatment. Luckily, my father was present and threatened to break the doctor in half if they let her die. Think about your children before you get complacent about your rights" **(Myra Hale)**

"In the early '60s my father wanted a vasectomy after having four children. The Dr. would NOT give it to him. My youngest sister was born with difficulties in '63. There must have been problems on both sides of the fence with some situations. There were for my dad." **(Anne Harris)**

"I have been a nurse for 37 years and in geriatrics for most of it. Some of the worst memories that my female residents had were of rape, illegal abortions, and spousal or child sexual assault at the hands of a family member or family friend. The only way to get them through it is to hold them while they relive these horrors that they lived through."
(Susan Bernard) Little Ferry, New Jersey
S Weeks Response: "Whenever I hear that females shouldn't get pregnant, that birth control is available, I think they must have never heard of rape or incest."

"When I was 19, I desperately tried to get birth control, but couldn't. Doctors would only prescribe "the pill" to married

156

women with the permission of their husbands. I nearly got thrown out of college, because pregnant women (even married women) were not deemed suitable to obtain an education. Abortions were impossible. So I married a guy I didn't even lie and had a child way before I was ready. When I was a girl, I almost lost my mother, who desperately needed an abortion to save her life. The child she was carrying died and turned septic. Still, my father had to get a court order to allow the doctor to save my mother's life. This is not ancient history. And I fear it will soon be repeated". **(Nancy Stevens Mendoza)**

"I was married with 3 children and I wanted a tubal ligation (sterilization) after the 3rd child. This was 1973 and I had to have my husband's approval for the procedure (I was 31.)" **(Alice Abel Kemp)** University of Georgia

"I had forgotten that contraceptives were illegal as I was married in '62 after they had become legal. I had two children, my mother -4, her mother -8, and her mother -12. Thanks for the reminder!" **(Marilyn Abraham)** Augustana College, Sioux Falls, S. D.

"Thank you so much for this historical reminder. On a talk show recently women were talking about having periods and the elder of the group mentioned the belts that went around us and held up the menstrual pad. The younger women had no idea what she was talking about. All they know are tampons" **(Colleen Welch)** Conservation Education Coordinator at NW Dept., Game & Fish

"In 1972 I was a student at WVU and engaged. I went to a woman OBGYN in Morgantown and got on the pill. Two of my friends went to the University health care service and also got on the pill, but they didn't realize the school would notify their parents". **(Bettey Kruger)** St. Mary's, Pennsylvania

Eugenics – Involuntary Sterilization

"I wish this article had included the forced sterilization of women in this country, in particular minority women and poor women. Native American women, especially full-blooded, were forcefully sterilized from 1970-1976 resulting in as many as 20%-50% of Native American women were forcefully sterilized by 1976. I can just imagine what would happen today if American women started to discover they were sterilized without giving permission, while undergoing another procedure, such as a C section. Some were forced to endure hysterectomies back in the 70's, just imagine if that happened today?

Today's women need to wake up. This stuff was still happening when I was a child. Women today have no idea what women from just a few decades ago had to endure just so the privileges of today could happen. Every single woman in the country needs to count her blessings and get involved in protecting the rights we do have, even if there is no desire to fight for the rest of our human rights. This isn't just about you....this is about your daughters and your granddaughters, your sisters, your nieces, your cousins. There are still many in our country (mostly wealthy white men, but not exclusively) who desire to see women return to being the property of her father and then her husband if/when she marries. I ask every woman out there to look long and hard in your mirrors and ask yourself, "am I content to live my life as the legal property of my father or my husband without any rights of my own? If you answer yes, please seek psychiatric help immediately. If your answer is no, then get out there and be heard, be seen, stand up for yourself and every woman in this country, to protect what is ours right now, before we lose it all. All of it. It will all start with one....if we let it." **(Dawn Moneyhan)**

"I read this comment, one of the first I received, and wondered if this could be true. Years ago when I moved to Chippewa Falls, Wisconsin, I had hear comments about this taking place at the Northern Center, located right outside of Chippewa Falls, once called the Wisconsin Home for the Feeble Minded. It opened in June of 1897. Dawn had listed two websites for references and I went to both of them. They seemed legit, but if I was going to publish this I wanted more. So I started looking. Was I in for a surprise!" **Sharon Weeks**

Coerced sterilization is a shameful part of America's history, and one doesn't have to go too far back to find examples of it. Used as a means of controlling "undesirable" populations – immigrants, people of color, poor people, unmarried mothers, the disabled, the mentally ill – federally-funded sterilization programs took place in 32 states throughout the 20th century. Driven by prejudiced notions of science and social control, these programs informed policies on immigration and segregation.

Beginning in 1909 and continuing for 70 years, California led the country in the number of sterilization procedures performed on men and women, often without their full knowledge and consent. Approximately 20,000 sterilizations took place in state institutions, comprising one-third of the total number performed in the 32 states where such action was legal.

"There is today one state," wrote Hitler, "in which at least weak beginnings toward a better conception [of citizenship] are noticeable. Of course, it is not our model German Republic, but the United States." [22]

Researcher Alex Stern, author of the new book _Eugenic Nation: Faults and Frontiers of Better Breeding in America_, adds:

"In the early 20th century across the country, medical superintendents, legislators, and social reformers affiliated with an emerging eugenics movement joined forces to put sterilization laws on the books. Such legislation was motivated by crude theories of human heredity that posited the wholesale inheritance of traits associated with a panoply of feared conditions such as criminality, feeblemindedness, and sexual deviance. Many sterilization advocates viewed reproductive surgery as a necessary public health intervention that would protect society from deleterious genes and the social and economic costs of managing 'degenerate stock'."

Eugenics was a commonly accepted means of protecting society from the offspring (and therefore equally suspect) of those individuals deemed inferior or dangerous.

Coerced sterilization is a shameful part of America's history, and one doesn't have to go too far back to find examples of it. Used as a means of controlling "undesirable" populations – immigrants, people of color, poor people, unmarried mothers, the disabled, the mentally ill – federally-funded sterilization programs took place in 32 states throughout the 20th century. Driven by prejudiced notions of science and social control, these programs informed policies on immigration and segregation.

As historian William Deverell explains in a piece discussing the "Asexualization Acts" that led to the sterilization of more than 20,000 California men and women, "If you are sterilizing someone, you are saying, if not to them directly, 'Your possible progeny are inassimilable, and we choose not to deal with that.'" According to Andrea Estrada at UC Santa Barbara, forced sterilization was particularly rampant in California (the state's eugenics program even inspired the Nazis.)

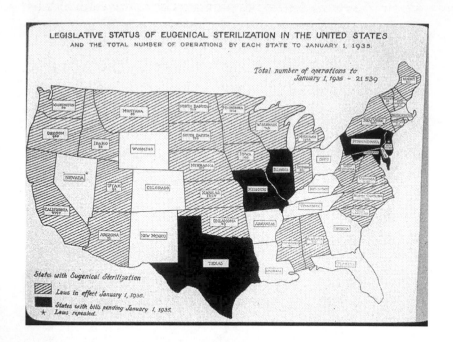

LEGISLATIVE STATUS OF EUGENICAL STERILIZATION IN THE UNITED STATES
AND THE TOTAL NUMBER OF OPERATIONS BY EACH STATE TO JANUARY 1, 1935.

Total number of operations to
January 1, 1935 - 21 539

States with Eugenical Sterilization

Laws in effect January 1, 1935.

States with bills pending January 1, 1935.
★ Laws repealed.

More recently, California prisons are said to have authorized sterilizations of nearly 150 female inmates between 2006 and 2010. This article from the Center for Investigative Reporting reveals how the state paid doctors $147,460 to perform tubal ligations that former inmates say were done under coercion.

But California is far from being the only state with such troubled practices. For a disturbing history lesson, check out this comprehensive database for your state's eugenics history. You can find out more information on state-by-state sterilization policies, the number of victims, institutions where sterilizations were performed, and leading opponents and proponents.

While California's eugenics programs were driven in part by anti-Asian and anti-Mexican prejudice, Southern states also employed sterilization as a means of controlling African American populations. "Mississippi appendectomies" was another name for unnecessary hysterectomies performed at teaching hospitals in the South on women of color as practice for medical students. This NBC news article discusses North Carolina's eugenics program, including stories from victims of forced sterilization like Elaine Riddick. A third of the sterilizations were done on girls under 18, even as young as 9. The state also targeted individuals seen as "delinquent" or "unwholesome." Gregory W. Rutecki, MD writes about the forced sterilization of Native Americans, which persisted into the 1970s and 1980s, with examples of young women receiving tubal ligations when they were getting appendectomies. It's estimated that as many as 25-50 percent of Native American women were sterilized between 1970 and 1976. Forced sterilization programs are also a part of history in Puerto Rico, where sterilization rates are said to be the highest in the world. [23]

Also see:
STERILIZED in the Name of Public Health | AJPH | Vol. 95 ... https://ajph.aphapublications.org/doi/full/10.2105/AJPH.200 4.041608

Sterilized in the name of public health: race, immigration ... https://pubmed.ncbi.nlm.nih.gov/1598326

Female Genital Mutilation

Key facts

- Female genital mutilation (FGM) involves the partial or total removal of external female genitalia or other injury to the female genital organs for non-medical reasons.
- The practice has no health benefits for girls and women.
- FGM can cause severe bleeding and problems urinating, and later cysts, infections, as well as complications in childbirth and increased risk of newborn deaths.
- More than 200 million girls and women alive today have been cut in 30 countries in Africa, the Middle East and Asia where FGM is concentrated (1).
- FGM is mostly carried out on young girls between infancy and age 15.
- FGM is a violation of the human rights of girls and women.
- WHO is opposed to all forms of FGM, and is opposed to health care providers performing FGM (medicalization of FGM).
- Treatment of health complications of FGM in 27 high prevalence countries costs 1.4 billion USD per year.

164

Female genital mutilation (FGM) comprises all procedures that involve partial or total removal of the external female genitalia, or other injury to the female genital organs for non-medical reasons.

The practice is mostly carried out by traditional circumcisers, who often play other central roles in communities, such as attending childbirths. In many settings, health care providers perform FGM due to the belief that the procedure is safer when medicalized[1]. WHO strongly urges health care providers not to perform FGM.

FGM is recognized internationally as a violation of the human rights of girls and women. It reflects deep-rooted inequality between the sexes, and constitutes an extreme form of discrimination against women. It is nearly always carried out on minors and is a violation of the rights of children. The practice also violates a person's rights to health, security and physical integrity, the right to be free from torture and cruel, inhuman or degrading treatment, and the right to life when the procedure results in death.

Types of FGM

Female genital mutilation is classified into 4 major types.

- **Type 1:** this is the partial or total removal of the clitoral glans (the external and visible part of the clitoris, which is a sensitive part of the female genitals), and/or the prepuce/ clitoral hood (the fold of skin surrounding the clitoral glans).
- **Type 2:** this is the partial or total removal of the clitoral glans and the labia minora (the inner folds of the vulva), with or without removal of the labia majora (the outer folds of skin of the vulva).

165

- **Type 3:** Also known as infibulation, this is the narrowing of the vaginal opening through the creation of a covering seal. The seal is formed by cutting and repositioning the labia minora, or labia majora, sometimes through stitching, with or without removal of the clitoral prepuce/clitoral hood and glans (Type I FGM).
- **Type 4:** This includes all other harmful procedures to the female genitalia for non-medical purposes, e.g. pricking, piercing, incising, scraping and cauterizing the genital area.

Deinfibulation refers to the practice of cutting open the sealed vaginal opening of a woman who has been infibulated, which is often necessary for improving health and well-being as well as to allow intercourse or to facilitate childbirth.

No health benefits, only harm

FGM has no health benefits, and it harms girls and women in many ways. It involves removing and damaging healthy and normal female genital tissue, and interferes with the natural functions of girls' and women's bodies. Generally speaking, risks of FGM increase with increasing severity (which here corresponds to the amount of tissue damaged), although all forms of FGM are associated with increased health risk.

Immediate complications can include:

- severe pain
- excessive bleeding (haemorrhage)
- genital tissue swelling
- fever
- infections e.g., tetanus
- urinary problems

166

- wound healing problems
- injury to surrounding genital tissue
- shock
- death.

Long-term complications can include:

- urinary problems (painful urination, urinary tract infections);
- vaginal problems (discharge, itching, bacterial vaginosis and other infections);
- menstrual problems (painful menstruations, difficulty in passing menstrual blood, etc.);
- scar tissue and keloid;
- sexual problems (pain during intercourse, decreased satisfaction, etc.);
- increased risk of childbirth complications (difficult delivery, excessive bleeding, caesarean section, need to resuscitate the baby, etc.) and newborn deaths;
- need for later surgeries: for example, the sealing or narrowing of the vaginal opening (Type 3) may lead to the practice of cutting open the sealed vagina later to allow for sexual intercourse and childbirth (deinfibulation). Sometimes genital tissue is stitched again several times, including after childbirth, hence the woman goes through repeated opening and closing procedures, further increasing both immediate and long-term risks;
- psychological problems (depression, anxiety, post-traumatic stress disorder, low self-esteem, etc.);

Who is at risk?

FGM is mostly carried out on young girls sometime between infancy and adolescence, and occasionally on adult women. More than 3 million girls are estimated to be at risk for FGM annually.

More than 200 million girls and women alive today have been subjected to the practice, according to data from 30 countries where population data exist. [23].

The practice is mainly concentrated in the Western, Eastern, and North-Eastern regions of Africa, in some countries the Middle East and Asia, as well as among migrants from these areas. FGM is therefore a global concern.

Cultural and social factors for performing FGM

The reasons why female genital mutilations are performed vary from one region to another as well as over time, and include a mix of sociocultural factors within families and communities. The most commonly cited reasons are:

- Where FGM is a social convention (social norm), the social pressure to conform to what others do and have been doing, as well as the need to be accepted socially and the fear of being rejected by the community, are strong motivations to perpetuate the practice. In some communities, FGM is almost universally performed and unquestioned.
- FGM is often considered a necessary part of raising a girl, and a way to prepare her for adulthood and marriage.
- FGM is often motivated by beliefs about what is considered acceptable sexual behaviour. It aims to ensure premarital virginity and marital fidelity. FGM is in many communities believed to reduce a woman's libido and therefore believed to help her resist extramarital sexual acts. When a vaginal opening is covered or narrowed (Type 3), the fear of the pain of opening it, and the fear that this will be found out, is expected to further discourage

168

extramarital sexual intercourse among women with this type of FGM.

- Where it is believed that being cut increases marriageability, FGM is more likely to be carried out.
- FGM is associated with cultural ideals of femininity and modesty, which include the notion that girls are clean and beautiful after removal of body parts that are considered unclean, unfeminine or male.
- Though no religious scripts prescribe the practice, practitioners often believe the practice has religious support.
- Religious leaders take varying positions with regard to FGM: some promote it, some consider it irrelevant to religion, and others contribute to its elimination.
- Local structures of power and authority, such as community leaders, religious leaders, circumcisers, and even some medical personnel can contribute to upholding the practice. Likewise, when informed, they can be effective advocates for abandonment of FGM.
- In most societies, where FGM is practiced, it is considered a cultural tradition, which is often used as an argument for its continuation.
- In some societies, recent adoption of the practice is linked to copying the traditions of neighbouring groups. Sometimes it has started as part of a wider religious or traditional revival movement.

A financial burden for countries

WHO has conducted a study of the economic costs of treating health complications of FGM and has found that the current costs for 27 countries where data were available totalled 1.4 billion USD during a one year period (2018). This amount is expected to rise to 2.3 billion in 30 years (2047) if FGM prevalence remains the same –

corresponding to a 68% increase in the costs of inaction. However, if countries abandon FGM, these costs would decrease by 60% over the next 30 years.

International response

Building on work from previous decades, in 1997, WHO issued a joint statement against the practice of FGM together with the United Nations Children's Fund (UNICEF) and the United Nations Population Fund (UNFPA).

Since 1997, great efforts have been made to counteract FGM, through research, work within communities, and changes in public policy. Progress at international, national and sub-national levels includes:

- wider international involvement to stop FGM;
- international monitoring bodies and resolutions that condemn the practice;
- revised legal frameworks and growing political support to end FGM (this includes a law against FGM in 26 countries in Africa and the Middle East, as well as in 33 other countries with migrant populations from FGM practicing countries);
- the prevalence of FGM has decreased in most countries and an increasing number of women and men in practicing communities support ending its practice.

Research shows that, if practicing communities themselves decide to abandon FGM, the practice can be eliminated very rapidly.

In 2007, UNFPA and UNICEF initiated the Joint Programme on Female Genital Mutilation/Cutting to accelerate the abandonment of the practice.

In 2008, WHO together with 9 other United Nations partners, issued a statement on the elimination of FGM to support increased advocacy for its abandonment, called: "Eliminating female genital mutilation: an interagency statement". This statement provided evidence collected over the previous decade about the practice of FGM.

In 2010, WHO published a "Global strategy to stop health care providers from performing female genital mutilation" in collaboration with other key UN agencies and international organizations. WHO supports countries to implement this strategy.

In December 2012, the UN General Assembly adopted a resolution on the elimination of female genital mutilation.

Building on a previous report from 2013, in 2016 UNICEF launched an updated report documenting the prevalence of FGM in 30 countries, as well as beliefs, attitudes, trends, and programmatic and policy responses to the practice globally.

In May 2016, WHO in collaboration with the UNFPA-UNICEF joint program on FGM launched the first evidence-based guidelines on the management of health complications from FGM. The guidelines were developed based on a systematic review of the best available evidence on health interventions for women living with FGM.

In 2018, WHO launched a clinical handbook on FGM to improve knowledge, attitudes, and skills of health care providers in preventing and managing the complications of FGM.

WHO response

In 2008, the World Health Assembly passed resolution WHA61.16 on the elimination of FGM, emphasizing the need for concerted action in all sectors - health, education, finance, justice and women's affairs.

WHO efforts to eliminate female genital mutilation focus on:

- strengthening the health sector response: developing and implementing guidelines, tools, training and policy to ensure that health care providers can provide medical care and counselling to girls and women living with FGM and communicate for prevention of the practice;
- building evidence: generating knowledge about the causes, consequences and costs of the practice, including why health care providers carry out the practice, how to abandon the practice, and how to care for those who have experienced FGM;
- increasing advocacy: developing publications and advocacy tools for international, regional and local efforts to end FGM, including tools for policy makers and advocates to estimate the health burden of FGM and the potential public health benefits and cost savings of preventing FGM [23]

Chapter VI

LBGTQ

From Original Article 2017
Gay Rights Marches *Again people were beaten and killed, (think Mathew Sheppard) even when not participating in marches, but while just trying to live their lives like people of color before them. Eventually gains were made and same-sex marriage was legalized in 2015 and couples were accorded the same rights and benefits as heterosexual couples. Acceptance is at an all time high and rising.*

For those of you too young to remember: Matthew Wayne Shepard, 22, was a gay American student at the University of Wyoming who was beaten, tortured, and left to die near Laramie on the night of October 6, 1998. He was taken by rescuers to Poudre Valley Hospital in Fort Collins, Colorado, where he died from severe head injuries six days later.

Suspects Aaron McKinney and Russell Henderson were arrested shortly after the attack and charged with first-degree murder following Sheppard's death. Significant media coverage was given to the murder and what role Shepard's sexual orientation played as a motive for the commission of the crime. The prosecutor argued that McKinney's murder of Shepard was premeditated and driven by greed. McKinney's defense counsel countered by arguing that he had only intended to rob Shepard but killed him in a rage when Shepard made a sexual advance toward him. McKinney's girlfriend told police that he had been motivated by anti-gay sentiment but later recanted her statement, saying that she had lied because she thought it would help him. Both McKinney and Henderson were convicted of the murder, and each of them received two consecutive life sentences.

Older groups such as the Mattachine Society, which was founded in southern California as a discussion group for gay men and had flourished in the 1950s, soon made way for more radical groups such as the Gay Liberation Front (GLF) and the Gay Activists Alliance (GAA). In addition to launching numerous public demonstrations to protest the lack of civil rights for gay individuals, these organizations often resorted to such tactics as public confrontations with political officials and the disruption of public meetings to challenge and to change the mores of the times. Acceptance and respect from the establishment were no longer being humbly requested but angrily and righteously demanded. The broad-based radical activism of many gay men and lesbians in the 1970s eventually set into motion a new, nondiscriminatory trend in government policies and helped educate society regarding this significant minority.

The event sparked the formation of scores of gay rights Shepard's murder brought national and international attention to hate crime legislation at both the state and federal level. In October 2009, the United States Congress passed the Matthew Shepard and James Byrd Jr. Hate Crimes Prevention Act (commonly the "Matthew Shepard Act" or "Shepard/Byrd Act" for short), and on October 28, 2009, President Barack Obama signed the legislation into law. Following her son's murder, Judy Shepard became a prominent LGBT rights activist and established the Matthew

174

Shepard Foundation. Shepard's death inspired films, novels, plays, songs, and other works. Wikipedia · Text under CC-BY-SA license [25]

This is a reason people march!

Stonewall Uprising

Stonewall riots, also called **Stonewall uprising**, series of violent confrontations that began in the early hours of June 28, 1969, between police and gay rights activists outside the Stonewall Inn, a gay bar in the Greenwich Village section of New York City. As the riots progressed, an international gay rights movement was born.

In 1969 the solicitation of homosexual relations was an illegal act in New York City (and indeed virtually all other urban centres). Gay bars were places of refuge where gay men and lesbians and other individuals who were considered sexually suspect could socialize in relative safety from public harassment. Many of those bars were, however, subject to regular police harassment.

One such well-known gathering place for young gay men, lesbians, and transgender people was the Stonewall Inn in Greenwich Village, a dark, seedy, crowded bar, reportedly operating without a liquor license. In the early morning hours of Saturday, June 28, 1969, nine policemen entered the Stonewall Inn, arrested the employees for selling alcohol without a license, roughed up many of its patrons, cleared the bar, and—in accordance with a New York criminal statute that authorized the arrest of anyone not wearing at least three articles of gender-appropriate

175

clothing—took several people into custody. It was the third such raid on Greenwich Village gay bars in a short period.

This time the people milling outside the bar did not retreat or scatter as they almost always had in the past. Their anger was apparent and vocal as they watched bar patrons being forced into a police van. They began to jeer at and jostle the police and then threw bottles and debris. Accustomed to more passive behaviour, even from larger gay groups, the policemen called for reinforcements and barricaded themselves inside the bar while some 400 people rioted. The police barricade was repeatedly breached, and the bar was set on fire. Police reinforcements arrived in time to extinguish the flames, and they eventually dispersed the crowd.

The riots outside the Stonewall Inn waxed and waned for the next five days. Many historians characterized the uprising as a spontaneous protest against the perpetual police harassment and social discrimination suffered by a variety of sexual minorities in the 1960s. Although there had been other protests by gay groups, the Stonewall incident was perhaps the first time lesbians, gays, and transgender people saw the value in uniting behind a common cause. Occurring as it did in the context of the civil rights and feminist movements, the Stonewall riots became a galvanizing force.

Stonewall soon became a symbol of resistance to social and political discrimination that would inspire solidarity among homosexual groups for decades. Although the Stonewall riots cannot be said to have initiated the gay rights movement as such, it did serve as a catalyst for a new generation of political activism. organizations, including the Human Rights Campaign, OutRage! (U.K.-based), GLAAD (formerly Gay and Lesbian Alliance Against Defamation), PFLAG (formerly Parents, Families and Friends of Lesbians and Gays), and Queer Nation. In 1999 the U.S. National Park Service placed the Stonewall Inn on the National Register of Historic Places, and in 2016 Pres. Barack Obama designated the site of the Stonewall uprising a national monument. The 7.7-acre (3.1-hectare) monument included the Stonewall Inn, Christopher Park, and the surrounding streets and sidewalks. In 2019, shortly before the 50th anniversary of the riots, New York City's police commissioner, James P. O'Neill, issued an apology on behalf of the police department saying, "The actions taken by the N.Y.P.D. were wrong—plain and simple." [26]

2013 Reauthorization of the Violence Against Women Act. The new bill extends coverage to women of Native American tribal land who are attached by non-tribal residents, as well as lesbians and immigrants.
The Violence Against Women Act established in 1994 was allowed to expire this year, 2020

Progress toward LGBTQ equality 'is a jagged line.' Here's what has changed over the past decade. (From USA Today February 2020)

In 2010, no states outlawed conversion therapy for LGBTQ minors, banned health insurers from excluding transgender-related coverage or offered gender neutral options on licenses and birth certificates.

Ten years later at the dawn of a new decade, roughly 20 states have these protections in place.

Breakthroughs? Or evidence of a plodding pace on the road to LGBTQ equality?

"It's both," said Ineke Mushovic, executive director of the Movement Advancement Project, which released a report Tuesday on the status of LGBTQ rights from 2010 to 2020.

"We have made a tremendous amount of progress understanding what LGBTQ people need to have a full opportunity to be productive workers, have equal access to health care, to go beyond the basics," she said. "But at the same time, in half the country, that progress has stalled out."

The report, which tracks nearly 40 LGBTQ-related policies and laws in all 50 states, Washington, D.C., and the five U.S. territories, does show significant strides:

• In 2010, 48% of LGBTQ people lived in "negative" policy states. By 2020, that number dropped to 20%.

• The number of people living in "medium" or "high" equality states increased dramatically from 6% in 2010 to nearly half, 46%, in 2020.

• In 2010, only 12 states and the district (D.C.) explicitly prohibited discrimination against LGBTQ people in employment, housing and public accommodations. By 2020, that number jumped to 21.

• In 2010, just five states and the district (D.C.) banned health care discrimination against LGBTQ people. In 2020, that number more than doubled to 13 states and the District of Columbia.

Treating trans youth a crime? <u>National firestorm on horizon as states consider criminalizing transgender treatments for youths</u>

Same-sex marriage ruling signals progress – then backlash

A landmark <u>Supreme Court ruling sanctioning same-sex marriage</u> in 2015 capped an evolution taking place in state legislatures and federal courts on LGTBQ relationships in the first half of the decade. In 2010, only 14 states and the district had some form of relationship recognition for same-sex couples. By 2020, marriage was the law of the land and included access to marriage-related parenting protections.

Bans on conversion therapy – a discredited practice of trying to change a young person's sexual orientation or gender identity – began to take root.

But midway through the decade, <u>backlashes also started to sprout</u>. Some targeted transgender people's rights. Many took the form of <u>religious exemption laws</u> that let people, churches and sometimes businesses cite religious beliefs as a reason not to enforce a law, such as declining to marry a same-sex couple or letting state-funded foster agencies refuse to place kids with LGBTQ parents.

The report by MAP, a think tank that maintains a database on laws affecting LGBTQ people, shows a split in the policy landscape in 2020: Nearly half – 46% – of the country lives in states earning "high" or "medium" grades for equality because of protections. But the other half – 45% – lives in states with "low" or "negative" rankings.

Advocates hope rulings in <u>three pivotal Supreme Court cases this year</u> on whether it's legal to fire workers because of sexual orientation or gender identity will cement a precedent for LGBTQ rights. They also will continue to press for passage of the Equality Act, which would make nondiscrimination a federal guarantee.

'We are not drag queens': For transgender people in 2019, a conflicted reality

But for now, LGBTQ people are at the mercy of a patchwork of state protections. "You could live in one state and move across the border and core pieces of your life could be in jeopardy," said Naomi Goldberg, MAP policy research director.

When we saw progress in marriage a decade ago, LGBTQ opponents realized that fight was over. All the rights and benefits that came along with marriage were solidified," Goldberg said. "But it was a strategic move on (opponents') part. Yes, you can go get married, but when you show up to get that license, we can say no – you have to go somewhere else."

'Shocking' numbers: Half of LGBTQ adults live in states where no laws ban job discrimination

In 2010, only one state had a religious exemption law. Now 13 states have those laws.

And more harmful bills are percolating. In 2020, MAP's database shows at least 121 anti-LGBTQ pieces of legislation in the mix in various states. Transgender young people take a particularly hard-hit: Fourteen states are weighing bills excluding transgender students from sports, and 11 have floated legislation that bans medical care for transgender minors, some even making treatment a crime.

And at least 14 states have three or more anti-LGBTQ bills on the docket.

Local laws help notch progress in Florida
Nadine Smith lives in Florida, where "Anita Bryant put us on the map in the worst possible way" in the 1970s with her

anti-gay crusades.

But Smith, the CEO and co-founder of civil rights group, Equality Florida, has seen a slow transformation in the state in recent years, mainly because cities and counties have moved the marker – much more so than the Legislature.

In 2010, Florida was ranked a "negative" equality state by MAP. Ten years later, it's a "low" equality state. "The people of Florida are absolutely moving in the correct direction," Smith said. "The majority of people are living in places where localities have passed nondiscrimination ordinances on sexual orientation and gender identity. Localities are showing leadership where the state has failed."

As LGBTQ people become more visible, attitudes shift and inspire change, Smith said. People "meet janitors, firefighters, accountants all living a life for themselves. Being out in everyday situations matters a great deal."

Life in rural America: Nearly 4 million LGBTQ people live in rural America, and 'everything is not bias and awful'
But the number of detrimental bills being weighed in the coming year in Florida – including one "horrific" piece of legislation that threatens doctors with up to 15 years of prison time for providing medical care to trans youths – loom large, she said. "To introduce legislation that would erode local policies in existence for more than a decade ... it's clear we are collateral damage."

Yet, Smith remains determined and optimistic. When she was growing up in the Panhandle, she had to trick a classmate into checking out a book that had gay themes from the library. Now her former high school has a gay alliance and there are anti-bullying policies.

Progress is "a jagged line. There's backlash, but sometimes it's like a rubber band. And we emerge from that backlash, growing much further."

In Colorado, bipartisan boost leads to inroads on equality

Daniel Ramos, executive director of One Colorado, has seen his state rocket up the road on equality in the 10 years since the LGBTQ advocacy group was founded. In 2010, MAP ranked the state "fair"; now it is a "high" equality state.

One Colorado focuses on amplifying LGBTQ voices in all parts of the state in an effort to educate and engage, he said. "One of the most powerful lessons we learned is the impact of sharing our own experiences by coming out. It's harder to hate someone you know or you love."

The state is home to some high-profile groups that oppose LGBTQ rights, yet Colorado has notched many advancements, such as a conversion therapy ban and accurate ID documentation, notably through bipartisan efforts, Ramos said. In 2018, Coloradoans elected their first openly transgender legislator and the country's first openly male gay governor.

"The challenge has been that issues are hyperpoliticized," Ramos said. "But for youths to experience less bullying should be a nonpartisan issue, for folks to access health care should be a nonpartisan issue."

Ramos, who grew up in the rural town of Sterling, recalls coming out at age 13. It was one year after college student Matthew Shepard's slaying in 1998, a gruesome incident that cast an unnerving spotlight on hate crimes against LGBTQ people.

"When I think of my upbringing to where we are today in one of the most LGBTQ-friendly states in the country, it's very exciting," he said. "We have been able to leverage the spirit of Colorado to come together to get things done – whether Democrat or Republican, with conservatives and with faith communities." [27]

Fallout from transgender slayings: What happens after a transgender woman is murdered? For family and friends, a long and agonizing search for closure.

2013 United States v Windsor 570 U.S. Supreme Court decides that a key part of DOMA, the law that restricts federal recognition of same-sex marriage, is unconstitutional because it violates the equal protection clause of the constitution.

Forward to 2020

Peter Paul Montgomery Buttigieg is an American politician and Afghanistan War veteran. He served as the mayor of South Bend, Indiana, from 2012 to 2020 and was a candidate for the Democratic nomination in the 2020 United States presidential election. He finished first in the Iowa Democratic Caucus in the pledged delegate count, though not in the popular vote count. Pete Buttigieg is the first openly gay married (Chasten Buttigieg) man to run for president of the U.S. He was recently confirmed as Secretary of Transportation.

Again, these are reasons people march!

Chapter VII

Education

From original article 2017: *One thing I want to point out, as I am going to discuss women's rights from more than a hundred years ago to 2017, is what I think these young women are missing. Women's history has been basically excluded from the classroom textbooks in public schools. Many people are not aware that a selected group of white men, a board of education in Texas, has been charged with the job of editing most of the history textbooks for decades. Their editing is final. (See Bill Moyers, "Messing with Textbooks," June 2012)*

This section of the article was roundly criticized as impossible. An article was printed in the Eau Claire, Wisconsin Leader-Telegram on September 15, 2018. **"Clinton voted out of curriculum"** Austin Texas. "History curriculum in Texas remembers the Alamo but could soon forget Hillary Clinton and Helen Keller. As part of an effort to "streamline" the social studies curriculum in Texas, the State Board of Education voted on Friday to change what students in every grade are required to learn in the classroom. They voted to remove several historical figures, including Hillary Clinton and Helen Keller. The board also voted to add back into the curriculum a reference to the "heroism" of the defenders of the Alamo, which had been recommended for elimination, as well as Moses' influence on the writing of the founding documents, multiple reference to "Judeo-Christian" values and a requirement that students explain how the "Arab rejection of the State of

Israel has led to ongoing conflict" in the Middle East. The vote Friday was preliminary. The board will take a final vote on these curriculum changes in November and can make further amendments before then."[28]

On November 18, 2018 the Leader-Telegram headline read **"New Texas curriculum keeps Hillary, Eleanor, Keller, Alamo"** Many were outraged over recommended exclusions Austin American-Statesman AUSTIN, Texas – Responding to concerns that Texas public school students would no longer learn about Hillary Clinton, Eleanor Roosevelt, Helen Keller and defenders of the Alamo, the State Board of Education took a final vote Friday to reject board-created working groups to remove the figures from social studies curriculum.........................Among the recommendations they made that received the most criticism from the interest groups were the removal of Keller, a disability rights advocate; Roosevelt, known for her fight for humanitarian causes, especially as first lady; Clinton, the first female presidential nominee of a major U.S. party; Women Air force Service Pilots, who flew planes in noncombat roles in World War II; and the defenders of the Alamo and a famous letter from William B. Travis pleading for more help at the Alamo. They also toned down the language of one of the more controversial elements of the social studies curriculum with lists slavery third among causes of the Civil war. ...." Tribune News Service.[29] From The Texas Tribune: **The Textbook Myth** "As the furor over the State Board of Education's ideological rewriting of social studies standards has exploded nationally in recent weeks, a primary narrative has emerged: that whatever 15 politicians in Texas (or at least the rightest-leaning half of them) decide will be published in textbooks nationwide for years to come.

That fear has already stoked a political backlash: One California state senator is drafting legislation to keep any hint of the Texas version of U.S. history out of California textbooks. "The de-emphasis on civil rights in so many areas — reducing the scope of Latino history, especially in a state like Texas — is just mind-boggling," said Adam Keigwin, chief of staff for San Francisco Democrat Leland Yee.

But Yee and his liberal-to-moderate contemporaries in other states need not fret, textbook industry experts say. **Though Texas has been painted in scores of** media reports **as the big dog that wags the textbook industry tail, that's simply no longer true — and will become even less true in the future,** as technological advances and political shifts transform the marketplace, said Jay Diskey, executive director of the **Association of American Publishers.** Diskey calls the persistent reports of Texas dominating the market an "urban myth." Yet the myth persists."[29]

Comments: Printed as received without editing.

"YES reversing women's rights by the Congress and this Trump administration is horrible. Though lest you forget or overlook the over 600 Sovereign Nations of Indigenous people of this land now called the US of America were not allowed to practice their religion legally until the Indian Religious Freedom Act of 1978!! The Trump Regime is hell bent on PRIVATIZING all the American Indian reservations now...where are all the American People standing up for these injustices?? WHERE? Call the White House Switch

Board 202-456-1414 and stop the Dakota Access Pipeline. which is on Treaty Lands at Standing Rock Reservation – home of the Dakota, Lakota, Nakota people of North Dakota- (and we will stand and fight to save your women rights not to be reversed in 2017, too." Signed **Michael Bryan** (**Patience Dogood**) singer, dressing room attendant. Gallery Queen at Dark Star Orchestra

"Thank you for gracious recall of a difficult past in American civil society. I remember being with a group of young women who were shocked in disbelief that in the 60's they could not open a checking account on their own without a man's approval." (**Sahar Taman**) University of Chicago

"Thank you so much for these reminders, Sharon. I marched on January 21st, and I"ll march again on April 22nd. I'm proud to be a female scientist and athlete and I'm ever so grateful to the women who marched before so that I could have the opportunities, education, and rights that I do today. I'm grateful for the parents who always supported me as a person. I don't think the idea that I was a woman EVER entered into a conversation about whether or not I could do something (other than being part of the church I grew up in but that's a whole other story). For those with children, please remember that such education/understanding begins at home for girls growing up to be women who KNOW they are equal". (**Jessico Jo**) Associate Professor at University of Wisconsin – Eau Claire

"I have two issues with your article. One, not all you women take one bit of their, as you call it, "status quo" lives

for granted and are educated on the sacrifices other have made for their freedoms. Also, if you came to this country ilegally and you refust to go through the proper legality of obtaining a green card or citizenship, then you should be deported." **(Toni Mae Nichols Roan)** Finlandia University
Sanda Currie from Delta Secondary School responded: "Did your ancestors come to this country "legally?" This country was stolen from the people who lived here. Read your history."

 Toni Mae Nichols Roan responded: "Not every US citizen's ancestors stole this country from the people who lived here. Read your history. My grandparents immegrated from England in the '40's and followed the legal process to become US citizens. They never came to this country illegally, therefore, your comment does not aply to me. And by the way, I love history and am already informed."
S Weeks Response: "I realize not all young women take their lives for granted, but many do. This was an effort to get to them."

"Women were required to give up their jobs as teachers when they got married". **(Liz Breadon)** Owner Practioner Liz Breadon Homeopathy.

Pat Seller Gillispie responded: "What kind of teachers? Every teacher I ever had, male and female, was married. From 1950-1961"

"I mentioned this to someone else...my mom was teaching in NH when she married in 1942...dad went to North Africa in WWII and mom had to find work in a war plant..no married teachers allowed. Same deal in PA after the war..so she

189

worked in Kaufman's Dept. store for years until they moved to Chicago in 1951." **(Jan Weems)**

Liz Breadon "PSG I am sorry that happened to your mom. I was born and raised in Georgia which some people always seemed to think if you lived in the South, you must be an uneducated hillbilly. I never had those problems, one of our 5th grade teachers taught while she was pregnant in '54. Guess I was just very fortunate."

"As a retired teacher I always mentioned some of the milestones in the march for equal rights for women. Besides Susan B. Anthony, Cady Stanton, I talked about the struggle of Elizabeth Blackwell becoming a physician. Also I told my students about my wife and the time she graduated from high school and wanted to go to college in 1960. Many of our universities were Notre Dame, U of Virginia. The careers she found open were house wife, mother, teacher, librarian and nurse." **(James McMann)**

"My high school counselor, in 1964, provided me with those same alternatives. I wanted to be a surgeon. He told me the most important title to put in front of my name was Mrs., not Dr. He said college would provide me with better choices for finding a good husband." **(GAIL DUSA)** Sacramento State

"I had a job in the late 60's, early 70's to pay for college. I was training a young man and when he got his first check he asked me to explain the deductions....he was making $50 more than me. I asked my boss how this was fair. He told me he had a family." **(Marsha Williams)** University of California, LA

"I agree most younger women don't know our history. I shared an info post (prepared by another group) with a few bullets of rights won in 1970's-'80's. Several young women were actually shocked about women not being able to take out a credit card in their own name until 1975. It was a learning moment for them. It's not their fault women were really. Women's history is glazed over with maybe a couple of pages if we're lucky. I think we just need to look for those moments to share a piece of our history." **(Audrey Demecke)** Senior Leadership Coach, Right Management

"There were separate job ads and women could only be secretaries or teachers, but had to quit if they were married and pregnant. Title 9 (IX) finally required Harvard to admit women. Supreme Court Justice Sandra Day O'Connor, who was second in her law school class couldn't get hired as a lawyer, only as a legal secretary, since she was a woman. Health care plans have been able to limit what health care women receive since "men were treated equally" since they didn't get maternity or contraception birth control coverage either." **(Maura Garcia)** Bryn Mawr College

"Bill Moyer's article was entitled "Messing with Texas Textbooks". It talks about the Texas board. They do not control all of the textbooks. **(Zizi Roberts)** Boynton Beach, Florida"

S Weeks Response "There are two newspaper articles and other links included in this book from 2018 regarding this subject. See the beginning of this chapter.

"As late as 1967 there was a seminar in the Harvard Graduate School of Education which was closed to women. It was on school administration. I was told women rarely became administrators (husband/family/children) and the worst part is that after hearing this, I just accepted it." **(Dianne Haley)** Oberin, Ohio
S Weeks Response: "I accepted some things like that, too. It's scary."

"The history of women fighting for their rights must be taught to young women so they can Maintain. The rights that women fought for in country. Thank you for this post. I will share it!" **(Chris Verberg)**

"My mother had a teaching certificate and taught for two years in Iowa, but when she got married in 1935, she had to quit. I had a four year college degree and teaching license in 1962. It was the policy of the school district in Oregon that when the teacher notified the district that she was pregnant, she would have to quit at the next holiday. That year when I notified the district that I was pregnant, the new assistant superintendent said, "If their mothers have babies, I don't know why their teachers can't!" I finished the school year." **(Arlene Dighton Williams)** University of Northern Iowa

"Lucy Bains Johnson, daughter of President Lyndon Johnson, was denied admission to Georgetown University. She had recently been married and was told she needed to pursue her career in the home, Not college." **(Corie Jones)**

"I am not that old, but as a retired school teacher and administrator, I can tell you that when I entered the teaching profession in 1979, the sexual harassment I endured in the teacher's lounge by many of the male teachers drove me to eating in the cafeteria with the middle school students. I was never taken seriously by my then principal. I worked twice as hard to prove myself as the men did in the school and I did not make the same rate of pay as they did for their lazy ethic. We have to keep fighting so things get better and do not go back to the way they were." **(Carol Sorvig)** Adjunt Faculty & U Supervisor at U of Redlands School of Edu

"While in college I took a woman's Study course. I was horrified to find out that back in the 1970's, in the state of Georgia, a woman that owned property had to give it to her husband when she married." **(Sandra Sundquist)** Northern Michigan University

"I am a retired teacher, and I remember how horrified I was to learn that Texas and California drive the content of textbooks. Their large population of kids means that publishers will kowtow to their wishes, and delete anything offensive." **(Lynda Brueseke Harman)** Retired from MCPS

"Basically I lost my reply saying that the young women need more momentum to back the passing of ERA! we fought hard to get it passed but the male lawmakers thought it would be better to pass legislation piecemeal or individual laws instead of giving us the whole enchilada` a (one amendment) that covers everything we need. We have laws

193

like maternity leave which varies by State. An ERA amendment would make the law the same for each state!!! I thank you, Sharon Weeks, for your history. I am a past member of the International Women's Year Committee (IWY) of the State of Connecticut and mandated by The USA State Dept. who invited me to serve with other women by the Carter Administration. There is a lot of history to IWY which held meetings in most USA states on women's issues and fed into the meetings in Houston Tx and Nairobi, Kenya. I hope that we as feminists will continue to make strides forward." **(Judy Guy)** University of New Haven

"I'm from New York. About 11+ years ago I moved to Texas only to find out their history books are way different! My kids and I grew up with details not taught or even available to Texas kids! Your summary was more than informative. It made me rethink things. Thanks much." **(Robin Sue Daminsky Contreras)** CUNY Lehman

"I've heard that Texas has watered down it's history texts to minimize progressive movements of the past. The gains made by women, gays, blacks, Indians & hispanics shouldn't be ignored." **(Phillip Schuster)** Biology Tutor at Mpls.Com

"Thank you for enlightening all of us. I was born in 1952 and have seen many changes for women's equality. You are right about today's young women. They probably think that it's always been this way. Let's get women's historical knowledge in history books" **(Denise Williams)** Community and Technical College

"Thank you for this overview. As a woman who came of age in the 60's, I was privileged to have a good historical basis. I knew that my Grandmother fought for the vote. I was blessed with fabulous professors at the University of Vermont. I passed this history to my daughter. I am appalled by the lack of historical context in the country today. We must stop reinventing the wheel! The lack of ALL clear history in our schools is appalling. If we obscure our past, we lose the perspective on which to build". **(Mary Campbell Caldwell)**

"Excellent summary and "alert." A few personal examples:
1959 - told I couldn't take HS chemistry as girls had no need for it.
1960 - told I couldn't take HS architectural drawing because girls could not be anything but nurses, secretaries or teachers.
1969-1970 was not allowed to continue to teach once my pregnancy showed." I was married.
1984- newly divorced and could not get gas or electric service restored to my home when my ex- husband took it out of his name. Needed a males name on the account. Etc. Etc. Etc. We are better off now, but there is still much to do!"
(Patti Rowe) Grand Valley State University (retired)

"Every girl needs to learn this history starting at about 12 years old and all thru high school....even if they won't do it in school, maybe as a summer school history credit...it's so sad this gets tossed out of the way as not important...it helped mold me into who I am and what my beliefs are.....great article." **(Teri Sickels)** Janesville, Wisconsin

"There is a wonderful movie that chronicles several generations of women of the same family titled, "A Will of their Own" and covers many of the issues and movements mentioned in this article. I always thought I should give copies to the next generation women in my family, so they could understand women's history. Now I realize how important it is for all young women of today. The DVD is available through Amazon." **(Sally Beatty Barto)** Snoqualmie, Washington

S Weeks Response: "(I checked, just do a search on Amazon for "A Will of Their Own" I did a search on Roku and didn't find it. It may also be available at public libraries.)"

"Show this to your daughters and sons. Mine never had history in school and wouldn't believe the content of this article. Beware. Laws and the people who write them are not always what you have been told." **(Claire Glaeser)** Townson University

"There is a children's book about Elizabeth Cady Stanton called "Elizabeth Leads the Way" and I always read it to my 2nd graders to show them what life was like for women before these brave women. It's also great for explaining the importance of voting since women at one time couldn't." **(Laura Elizabeth)** 2nd Grade teacher

"I tell young women this every day. We didn't do them any favors letting them think that their rights were forever, we forgot to tell them about the struggle, about the oppression, about the disrespect. Remind every young woman that these rights were not free or easy and the challenges go on. Guard your equality and stand up for what you have inherited from others. This is one slippery slope!!" **(Barbara Hersey-Scully)** EHS Advisor at OSI Occupational Service, Inc.

"Thanks for the lesson. I am 67 and remember the 60's. I was discouraged to major in science! I am stubborn nd I resisted. I have a Ph.D in Microbiology and have taught at the university for over 25 years! I remind my women students to study history....freedom is not a permanent condition. Do not be complacent." **(Judith Chapin Kjelstrom)** Director of Biotechnology Program at UC Davis

"I found out some of this information a while back by watching my favorite tv series Cosmos. There was a story about many famous women that I had never heard about. I was blown away that I had never heard about them." **(Danny Curlin)** Weimar, CA

"Your message about complacency is well take and appreciated. And you did a lovely job summarizing the progress of women's rights in the U.S. But I'm a 70 year old female Californian, educated at Portland State U and the U of Oregon. I can't remember when Women's Studies weren't covered in the schools at home. Is it seriously possible that in some parts of our great nation females are reading history books written by men who exclude women? Or is this just your experience in some part of the U.S. with which I am unfamiliar? Trying to load your argument with a seriously flawed view of women's studies in the United States doesn't help your case. It detracts. I strongly urge you to delete that in the future if you hope to be taken seriously. The United States as a whole isn't Chippewa Falls." **(Pat Todd)**

Eileen Davis, Cofounder at Women-Matter.org responds: "Yes it is. California is not the south, the midwest. I hail from N.J. and now live in Virginia. What my daughters know about Women's history came from me - not taught in schools, but "the war of northern aggression" is."

S Weeks Response: "**Eileen Davis**, Thank you again. There are news reports included in this book from 2018 that cover the deletions from textbooks re: women's history, and because of the internet and the availability of news to travel fast, a follow-up article about the topics that were replaced due to public opinion."

"I was taught these things in history class and via textbooks. I've heard the stories from my femail relatives, colleagues, and friends. Us young women are not as ignorant as you paint us to be." **(Chole Huber)**

S Weeks Response: "You thought I painted you as ignorant? How sad. There are lots of women who were not aware of the history of women. The article was titled, "What Young Women May Not Know." It was for the women who might not!"

"I am only 57 years old and girls in Fairmont, West Virginia at East Park were not allowed to wear pants. I walked to school every day it was cold. We have had to fight for rights the younger generation takes for granted". **(Sheri Sauro)**

"Marvelous piece so important to inform you women of women's struggle for human rights. I took it upon myself, when as a mature student, I discovered that many of the young women students weren't aware even of the progress made during the sixties. I felt it was my duty to point out that for instance maternity leave was not available when my first child was born and consequently, my job was lost! The young women were shocked as they had taken this right for granted!"
(Deirdre Houston) IT Sligo, Ireland

"History books until the 1970's and 80's only told about the women who were "nice" when demanding their rights. They chose to leave out those like Alice Paul for example. This is an important article for the younger generation to read and internalize. I do object, however, to the statement that the gains made can be done away with one swipe of a pen. The legislative branch, executive brand and judicial branch all have a role to play in changing a law. That does not mean we don't have to be vigilant and that there are not present inequities that still need to be changed, but it is not quite as simple as "the swipe of a pen." **(Kristie Pitts)** Teacher, Canyons School District
S Weeks Response: "Most of those laws are state laws and removable much more easily than a federal law. The Equal Rights Amendment meant as an amendment to the Constitution was never ratified. Check the end of the article regarding this."

"Should be required reading, to be informed is to be strengthened, we will need to be strong to save the gains that were made in the past, from the possible ravages of the future." **(Rudy Robertson)** Charlottesville, Virginia

"I think women are at least aware of this. I've had men tell me that this is false." **(Pat Blake)** Witchita, Kansas

S Weeks Response: "Apparently all women are not aware of this as I have had 4,600 responses and many say they weren't, and if they were, not aware of all of it. That is why I wrote the article. If men are telling you this is false, I suggest you go to the internet and check for yourself."

"I cannot understand why any woman would support Trump. I do know that no women in my family supported him or his crazy sidekick Pence. Education is so important to all people. We all need to stand strong together." **(Bill Atchison)** American Airlines

"This is real. The men from Texas must be stopped from deleting Women's History. Where do we start?" **(Bonnie J. Oliphint)** Real Estate Agent/Kalstar Realty Services

"Very good! should be distributed in schools, but ALSO IN CHURCHES!" **(Eva Dehmel)** Freie Universitaet Berlin/Tuebingen/Muenchen

"This is a very important summary and should be taught in every high school. People have forgotten are just not aware or just never knew. Stop looking at your phones and pay attention. As it is said, "Freedom is NOT Free." **(Arleen Larzelere)** P.A. at Renee Richards, MD PC

"My mother, born in Louisiana in 1907, was not sent to school after fourth grade. Many years later, I, her daughter with two master's degrees, insisted on some explanation for

200

her lack of education. All she could come up with was, "It was just not expected."" **(Frances Fuller)** Publisher, International Mission Board

"I am embarrassed that I didn't know some of this. But then, as the author notes, the textbook industry is controlled by a few. How do we change that?" **(Gregory Gaiser)** Trainer at Hakomi Institute Southwest

"You might be interested in: Assigned by the US Government, in 1946, Gen. MacArthur, then head of the Japanese Occupation Authority, was given the task of writing a constitution for Japan. He assigned the task to a 22 year old naturalized American citizen, Beate Sirota Gordon. She was told to use the US Constitution as a model. She did, but she added two striking simple but powerful clauses into the modern Japanese Constitution. These clauses stipulate equality among the sexes as well as civil rights for women involving marriage, money and family. Never widely known in her home country, she later became a well-known, decorated figure in Japan for her path breaking efforts. In other words: the Japanese Constitution has an equal rights clause. Ours does not, despite mighty efforts to introduce one." **(Sue J. Acocks)** Ferris State University

"Talk about history books....never once in all my years as a student or a teacher did I ever hear about the three talented mathematicians that were responsible for getting John Glenn off the ground. They were doubly discriminated against for their race and sex! **(Margaret J. Wergley)**

"Brava Sharon Weeks for detailing our struggles so well. I remember reading the Little Foxes years ago by Lilian Hellman and wondering how Regina, the title character,

201

could be so heartless and then I began to research women in the south, which led to property rights and they had none unless a father specifically put it in his will that his daughter would inherit his estate. Unfortunately, many of those wills were contested by male heirs. In most cases the property was left to the sons or to the husband of a daughter. Of course none of this was ever covered in any history books in schools." **(Dana DeMartino)**

"My wife had to leave her teaching job at semester when she was 7 months pregnant with no offer to return after the birth, 1972-1973. Until a girl from a good family became PG, who had some connections and wanted to graduate. Girls who were found to be PG were suspended from school. A young man who fathered 2 and had a 3rd on the way graduated." **(David A. Van Lieshout)**

"This is really great and very well thought. I appreciate your post immensely! Your words are very motivational and timely as we all are having to fight to keep what is good in the world right now with this administration and Congress, it would see. However, maybe I can offer some words of encouragement here. I was reading this article out loud to my 13 year old son who is in 8th grade and he told me he has learned quite a bit about women's rights in his middle school. He said he's studied women's history with regard to suffrage rights and ownership rights as well as the fact that women had very little rights and "say" over their own lives at an earlier time, not so long ago in history. I was extremely happy to hear this, of course, because he had not mentioned it before. I'm sure this information is available in the schools because of these battles throughout history by others who fought to make it so." **(Lulie Landoll**

Henerson) Hospice RN Case Manager, Ohio Living Home Health & Hospice

"Thank you for a great article, not just for young women. Maybe you would be interested to know that Title IX was a landmark legislation of Congresswoman Patsy Mink of Hawaii. She was a staunch supporter of women's rights, knowing first-hand that most women in Hawaii and

elsewhere worked as hard or harder than men. **(Alyce Dodge)** Honolulu, Hawaii **S Weeks Response** Thank you for that information.

"In the 1960's, girls were still being told; "you shouldn't bother going to college", "women can't be an engineer/doctor/scientist", we won't interview a woman - can't have a woman on the refinery/plant/machine floor', "you can't be a field geologist where you'll have to funk with men", "engineering aide? the boss must have made a mistake-can't have looked at the box for 'male or female'."" **(Louette McInnes)** Western High School (Baltimore)

"Thank you so much for bringing this problem to the forefront. It needed to be said. I tried my best to impart this knowledge to young people during my 36 years as an educator, making sure, especially during Women's History month, that the accomplishments of our unsung heroines were acknowledged and extensively studied. But not all educators take the time to fill in what school textbooks leave out. I wrote grants to get the money to fund my classroom with biographies about women who impacted our country, but sadly those courageous women are nowhere to be found in our history books. There are so many wonderful products available now, women's history playing cards with detailed facts about each person along with their contributions and areas of expertise. There are now a plethora of books on all educational levels, coloring books, paper dolls, even books about the women who fought during wartime. (Some going back to the Civil War.) When teachers read the Midnight Ride of Paul Revere to their students in April, they need to also include **Sybil Ludington** who rode further than Revere and was only 16 years old. My generation of teachers is now retiring and the next generation of educators MUST let girls and boys know that women fought and died along with men for the rights people have today. (Rights now taken for granted.) Things will not change for women in this country until educators value the roles women played in history. School systems need to extend the study of our foremothers from one month to the entire school year! The ignorance on this subject is enormous and it is simply because it is not being taught in schools across our country. That needs to change. Those of us who are old enough to remember what things were like in the 60's and 70's understand how much things have changed. I was a young divorced mother in 1975 and many schools would not hire me simply because I was divorced." **(Lesley Kluchin)** Sunrise, FL

"We all have individual experiences good and bad. We cannot apply our individual experience broadly as if it were proof of something one way or the other. The fact is that the laws, the workplace, financial institutions had horrific rules about women not being able to get their own accounts, healthcare, job, etc. without a male's signature. That doesn't change because one woman got a card in the 60's and another didn't. We are trying to change laws that keep women down, and resist change of all the legal and social progress that has been made for women,   I'm in my late fifties and around 1972, when I was 14 dreaming of being a chemical engineer I was told by my parents I should be an executive secretary and I was going NOT going to college because my brothers (younger) were being sent to prep school (St. Andrews and Choate) and college (Tufts and Stanford). Now I am an attorney and I had to work and pay my own way to get into college and grad school. Zero help. So let's come together and stop this. Treating women as less is still alive and well today. Just look at the news." **(Carrie Lilley)**

"My daughters formed a powerful women's group in their early 20's....20 years ago. It's still very viable today. The studied women's issues and are great examples of great women!" **(Charlotte Shapiro)** Boston College

"As retired professional woman, I know the path we've followed, but I also know that we are still behind in wages, respect, honors, etc. I have a Ph.D. and in a group of colleagues, the men are invariably referred to by others as "doctor" while I am called by my first name. I am also asked to take notes about the meeting. Something is wrong he". **(Shelby Morrison)** University of South Florida

"Well said. I had no idea it was men in Texas who decided on the content of text books". **(Katherine Cole Koch)** Case Western Reserve University School of Medicine

"This is so true. My hair stylist couldn't believe abortion could be illegal. She has no real understanding of Watergate, the draft or Vietnam. It's sad that when I tell women that they have a moral imperative to vote because of what the women endured to get the vote they look at me like I'm crazy. Likewise when I'm asked what sport I played in high school I laugh. Women's athletics didn't exist when I was in high school." **(Jeanne Clemens)** *See Chapter III, Title IX

"Thank you for this. People are so 'surprised' when stories like "<u>Hidden Figures</u>" appears in our lexicon. Because the tainted books we call history books in our education system have left out many accomplishments and historical breakthrough by women and minorities. It's as shameful as the way we treat the Native American Nations. As both of those shameful activities continue today. Hopefully, this will be shared and continued to be shared for a long time.....yes, the swipe of a pen can be the Sword to Damocles." **(Cathy Steffanci Sikorski)** Self employed

"Lately, I have also been thinking we failed our younger people, by not telling them how bad it was. I suppose we thought they would just know. Civil rights, women's rights, human rights, children's rights, but we must include the ecology. We think they knew how bad it was, turns out they don't. They were not there. I am guilty of not telling them. I regret not telling them. We can't change the past, so we must change the future." **(Annie Eash)** Perdue University

"Phenomenal summary. Very important. Very well-written. I hold a degree in US History and always had my students look at these issues in an age appropriate context. Many were incredulous that my Mom's dear friend, a WWII veteran with a Purple Heart for horrific injuries sustained when the hospital ship on which she was serving was kamikazed in the So. Pacific just weeks before VJ Day, was denied her Cal. Vet. Loan benefit to buy a house in her hometown of Fresno. Why? SHE WAS A WOMAN,

UNATTACHED TO ANY MAN. Never married. Father deceased. The year was 1955. Helen had a great job as a nurse in SF. Went home to Fresno as often as possible. Wanted a real home for her aging Mother, an Armenian immigrant who had fled her home country when violent hostilities erupted there in the early 1900's. This denial of Cal.Vet. loan benefits happened in MY LIFETIME. Never forget the struggle for equality for ALL continues and demands of each of us constant vigilance!" **Cathleen A. Guthrie)** San Francisco State University

"One of the texts I use in my women's lit class in Bangledesh is The Handmaid's Tale; my students are always shocked as to how relevant it is to life here today...and possibly to the near -future scenario in the US." **(Razia Sultana Khan)** University of Nebraska, Lincoln

"Thank you so much for this. I am a young woman, 26, craving knowledge...I'm lucky that I live with my 70 year old cousin, Dixie, age offers me wisdom on the daily...this speaks to me. I recently went to Pakistan by myself and stayed with a woman and her school. I got to see first hand oppressed women. What you speak of is so real. I might go back again, but I know what it takes to be careful. Can I please share your blog on www.WorldPulse.com if I give you full credit? I feel this is so important for everyone in the world to read, especially developing countries. So many women all over the world are fighting- you can hear their stories at WorldPulse—"**(Malee Kenworthy)** CAN at Healthcare

Response S Weeks: "Yes, Please share it as much as you can. And thank you so much for your comments."

"I learned more about women's history while reading "The Secret History of Wonder Woman" than I learned in 20 years of school. This needs to change. Women were alive in the past and we were doing stuff. Important stuff!" **(Heather Quellette-Cygan)** Belmont, New Hampshire

"This is frightful. I remember doing a research project in High School, "Women as a Minority in America". I wish I had kept it, but my teacher asked if she could keep it. I was honored to have her request that she keep it. This was back in 1980. All my research was done in libraries with card catalogs...lol " **(Beth Sargent)** Vice Present (JV Investment Systems)

"Women's history has definitely NOT been excluded from school books. I am half your age and remember most of the dates and information listed above. As a woman I am extremely grateful and proud of the women that fought this fight for me and others. However, I don't understand what women are marching about today. It is not for the memory of those before. It is for the supposed rights that we do not have now. We have the same rights as men in the United States. If someone wants to protest, I understand standing up for the atrocities that go on with women in countries like Saudi Arabia. (Which is why so many people are against Sharia law here.) Let's have some perspective and be grateful. American women are extremely blessed. The Mexican comment has to do with ILLEGAL immigration (BREAKING THE LAW) which has nothing to do specifically with women's rights. And I'm sorry, but abortion kills millions of women! So, all women are not for it." **(Tannette Monaco Knox)** Long Beach State
S Weeks Response: "Women's history has been excluded

from many textbooks. Women are marching today to remind people that even though they have many rights, they can easily be lost. Very easily lost. Please refer to Eau Claire Leader-Telegram articles from 2019 regarding textbook omissions at the beginning of this chapter."

"A wonderful summary for young women and young men particularly in high school. I think if more discussion on this topic as historical information with guidance in the classroom, perhaps the status quo of the young would bring about thoughtful thinking above how they got all the freedoms they enjoy, but could make ever better. Thanks for writing this commentary." **(Pat Duni DeVono)** North Canton, Ohio

"I am a white male and I am a history teacher. I DO teach all of the above mentioned topics in this article. Not every white male is a horrible person - so please quit villifying them - the more you do the more uphill your climb will be." **(RobConrad)**
S Weeks Response: "Thank you for your comments. I do not think, though, that most women think every white male is a horrible person."

"Thank you for this overview. As a woman who came of age in the 60's, I was privileged to have a good historical basis. I knew that my Grandmother fought for the vote. I was blessed with fabulous professors at the University of Vermont. I passed this history to my daughter. I am appalled by the lack of historical context in the country today. We must stop reinventing the wheel! The lack of ALL clear history in our schools is appalling. If we obscure our past, we lose the perspective on which to build." **(Mary Campbell Caldwell)**

"We are in grave danger with Trump. Without history or literature there is no perspective. America does not read. Complacency born of ignorance has led us to this dire place. "Give him a chance?" Saddest and most ignorant horrible thing people can say." **(Mathew Friedman)** Sales/Owner David Friedman & Sons

Please see Chapter III Title IX for news article on Betsy DeVos Title IX changes recommending making a fairer process for accused students and their schools. Advocates for survivors say DeVos' changes would roll back the progress for End Rape on Campus. Full article in Chapter III.

In addition to a comment regarding **Luci Baines Johnson**, the Washington Post printed the following:

"The question that changed the course of her life was asked in the solarium of the White House. It was 1965 and Luci Baines Johnson, the president's daughter, was looking at her boyfriend. He had just asked her to marry him. She could say yes. She could commit to him. She loved him, after all. Or she could continue her courses at Georgetown University, where she was studying to become a nurse. And that, she loved, too.

Doing both was not an option. Georgetown had a policy that forbade nursing students — all of whom were women — from marrying. At 19 years old, after just two semesters of school, Johnson chose marriage. She never received a degree from Georgetown. That is, until Saturday, when she was invited back to campus to serve as commencement speaker for Georgetown's School of Nursing and Health Studies. Fifty-two years after she dropped out of college, Johnson, 70, was awarded an honorary doctorate."

S Weeks

Chapter VIII

Employment

1873 Bradwell v. Illinois, 83 U.S> 130 (1872): The U.S.
Supreme Court rules that a state has the right to exclude
a married woman (Myra Colby Bradwell) from
practicing law.

1908 Muller v State of Oregon, 208 U.S. 412 (1908): The
U.S Supreme Court upholds Oregon's 10 hour workday
for women. The win is a two-edged sword: the protective
legislation implies that women are physically weak.

Triangle Shirtwaist Factory fire - Wikipedia

The Triangle Shirtwaist Factory fire in the Greenwich Village neighborhood of Manhattan, New York City, on March 25, 1911, was the deadliest industrial disaster in the history of the city, and one of the deadliest in U.S. history.

The fire caused the deaths of 146 garment workers – 123 women and girls and 23 men – who died from the fire, smoke inhalation, or falling or jumping to their deaths. Most of the victims were recent Italian and Jewish immigrant women and girls aged 14 to 23; of the victims whose ages are known, the oldest victim was 43-year-old Providenza Panno, and the youngest were 14-year-olds Kate Leone and Rosaria"Sara"Maltese.

The factory was located on the 8th, 9th, and 10th floors of the Asch Building, at 23–29 Washington Place, near Washington Square Park. The 1901 building still stands today and is now known as the Brown Building. It is part of and owned by New York University.

Because the doors to the stairwells and exits were locked (a then-common practice to prevent workers from taking unauthorized breaks and to reduce theft), many of the workers who could not escape from the burning building jumped from the high windows. The fire led to legislation requiring improved factory safety standards and helped spur the growth of the International Ladies' Garment Workers' Union (ILGWU), which fought for better working conditions for sweatshop workers. [29]

The building has been designated a National Historic Landmark and a New York City landmark.
Wikipedia · Text under CC-BY-SA license

Triangle shirtwaist factory fire, fatal conflagration that occurred on the evening of March 25, 1911, in a New York City sweatshop, touching off a national movement in the United States for safer working conditions.

The fire—likely sparked by a discarded cigarette—started on the eighth floor of the Asch Building, 23–29 Washington Place, just east of Washington Square Park. That floor and the two floors above were occupied by the Triangle Waist Company, a manufacturer of women's shirtwaists (blouses) that employed approximately 500 people. The flames, fed by <u>copious</u> cotton and paper waste, quickly spread upward to the top two floors of the building. Fire truck ladders were only able to reach six stories, and the building's overloaded fire escape collapsed. Many workers, trapped by doors that had been locked to prevent theft, leapt from windows to their deaths.

The 129 women and 17 men who perished in the 18-minute conflagration were mostly young European immigrants. It took several days for family members to identify the victims, many of whom were burned beyond recognition. Six of the victims, all interred under a monument in a New York City cemetery, were not identified until 2011 through research conducted by an amateur genealogist. A citywide outpouring of grief culminated on April 5, 1911, in a 100,000-strong procession behind the hearses that carried the dead along Fifth Avenue; thousands more observed the memorial gathering.

Though the owners of the factory were indicted later that month on charges of manslaughter, they were acquitted in December 1911; the owners ultimately profited from inflated insurance claims that they submitted after the tragedy. However, the uproar generated by the disaster led to the creation of the Factory Investigating Commission by the New York state legislature in June. Over the following year and a half, members of the commission visited factories, interviewed workers, and held public hearings. The commission's findings ultimately led to the passage of more than 30 health and safety laws, including factory fire codes and child labour restrictions, and helped shape future labour laws across the country. [30]

Deplorable Working Conditions

The fire, says Paul F. Cole, director of the American Labor Studies Center, "awakened a nation to the dangerous and deplorable conditions that many workers faced on a daily basis."

The disaster's causes were complex. In the early 1890s, immigrants from Italy and Eastern Europe came to the United States in search of a better life, but instead often found themselves in places such as the Triangle Waist Company, where they worked 12-and-a-half-hour days for $6 a week, according to an AFL-CIO history of the fire. They had to supply their own needles, thread, irons and sometimes, even their own sewing machines.

Working conditions were so bad that the women didn't even have access to a bathroom in the building, and doors were locked so that they couldn't go outside and slow down production. And though the place was filled with highly flammable materials, there was little attention paid to fire prevention.

Discontent over wages and working conditions at Triangle and the city's other garment factories led tens of thousands of workers to strike in 1909, seeking concessions such as a 20 percent pay hike and a 52-hour week, as well as safer working conditions. Most of the factory owners quickly settled, but Triangle's owners resisted the demands. When the strike ended in February 1910, workers went back to their jobs without a union agreement, according to the AFL-CIO history.

"Triangle was the most hostile of the owners to the union," explains Richard Greenwald, historian and dean of the College of Arts and Sciences at Fairfield University and author of a 2011 book, _The Triangle Fire, Protocols Of Peace And Industrial Democracy In Progressive Era New York_. "They moved production out of NYC in 1909 to avoid the strike, hired thugs to beat writers and most likely bribed the police to arrest strikers."

> **1937 U.S. Supreme Court upholds Washington State's minimum wage laws for women.**

Triangle Factory's Fire Safety: Empty Water Buckets

On the afternoon of March 25, a Saturday, 500 people were working in Triangle's factory, which occupied three floors in a building that had been built just 10 years before. Court testimony later placed the blame for the blaze on a fire that started in a fabric scrap bin on the eighth floor, which probably was ignited by a discarded cigarette, shortly before the factory's 4 pm closing time.

Triangle had water buckets in place for extinguishing fires, a common practice in garment factories at the time. But as one worker, Mary Domsky-Abrams, later recalled in an early 1960s interview with author Leon Stein, the buckets were empty. "On that particular morning, the day of the tragedy, I remarked to my colleagues that the buckets were empty, and that if anything were to happen, they would be of no use," she said.

Another worker, Cecilia Walker Friedman, who worked on the ninth floor, said that she was ready to leave work when she looked to the window and saw flames. Everyone around her started to scream and holler, but many were hindered in getting away. "The girls at the machines began to climb up on the machine tables, maybe because it was that they were frightened or maybe they thought they could run to the elevator doors on top of the machines," Friedman said. "The aisles were narrow and blocked by the chairs and baskets. They began to fall in the fire.

Firefighters eventually found a six-foot-high pile of bodies jammed up against a door to the back stairway, according to the *New York Tribune.*

Friedman herself somehow made it to the elevator, only to watch as the elevator car went down the shaft, leaving the door open. Desperate, she wrapped a decorative muff around her hands, leaped into the shaft and grabbed the elevator cable, sliding all the way to the bottom. The impact broke her arm and finger, and she suffered a head injury and a burn that stretched the length of her body. But she survived.

Others weren't so lucky. The fire escape bent under the weight of workers trying to flee. Some workers waited at the windows for help, only to watch in dismay as firefighters' too-short ladders couldn't reach them. Faced with being burned alive, some workers chose to leap—sometimes in twos and threes—to their deaths, according to a 2011 *New York Times* retrospective. The fire didn't destroy the building itself, and by sunset, police and firemen were laying out bodies on the sidewalk. [31]

From the Zinn Education Project 2014   The   impact women have made in labor history is often missing from textbooks and the media despite the numerous roles women have played to organize, unionize, rally, document, and inspire workers to fight for justice. From championing better workplace conditions to cutting back the 12-hour day to demanding equal pay across racial lines, these are just a few of the women who have contributed to the labor movement: Louise Boyle, Hattie Canty, May Chen, Jessie de la Cruz, Elizabeth Gurley Flynn, Emma Goldman, Velma Hopkins, Dolores Huerta, Mother Jones, Mary Elizabeth Lease, Clara Lemlich, Anna LoPizzo, Luisa Moreno, Agnes Nestor, Pauline Newman, Lucy Parsons, Ai-jen Poo, Frances Perkins, Rose Pesotta, Florence Reece, Harriet Hanson Robinson, Fannie Sellins, Vicky Starr, Emma Tenayuca, Carmelita Torres, Ella May Wiggins and Sue Cowan Williams.

https://www.zinnedproject.org/materials/women-in-labor-history/   Visit this website to read brief bios on 28 women listed above.   Also visit the And Still I Rise website that features Black women labor leaders women who had an impact on women in labor history like Lucy Parsons and Hatty Canty: Legendary African-American unionist Hattie Canty migrated to Las Vegas from rural Alabama. In contrast to the AFL-CIO's George Meany, who bragged that he had never been on a picket line, Canty was one of the greatest strike leaders in U.S. history. Her patient leadership helped knit together a labor union made up of members from 84 nations.

Comments: Printed as received without editing.

"I was employed by the great state of Ohio in the early 1970's and also was not allowed to wear anything but dresses to work! I was part of a group of women that formed a committee to change that rule, which we did! It still amazing to me, looking back, that we actually had to do that!" (**Betsy McCune**) Ohio State U)

1924 Radice v. New York, a New York case, upholds a law that forbade waitresses from working the night shift but made an exception for entertainers and ladies' room attendants.

1974 Cleveland Board of Education v. LaFleur, 414 U.S. 632 (1974) determines it is illegal to force pregnant women to take maternity leave on the assumtion they are incapable of working in their physical condition.

"I worked hard at my current profession and I actually make more that some of my male peers, bc of my experience, education and work ethic. Why should I make as much as a male if I didn't work for it? Life isn't about getting handed things bc you feel like you are entitled to them. That's exactly what is wrong with this country. I pay for feminine products bc I am biologically different from a man, that's the science behind it. I don't feel snorted (shortened?) bc of it. I feel honored bc the need for the feminine products means I can have children and create life. And I'm okay with that, it's a beautiful thing and I feel lucky that I am a woman for that. I knew about the vast majority of those facts bc I have google and smart phone and I know how to use them. Forgive me if I am "complacent" with my lot in life and I don't worry for my daughters future. Maybe if those worried about it did something to improve besides marching on Washington they wouldn't need to march." (**Courtney Marie Burge)**

"Interesting article, thanks for letting us have all this info. I had an experience in 1975 where I was a supervisor over a man and when I questioned why he was paid $10,000 more than me, I was told he had more experience which was crap as he and I both graduated from college with the same degree the same year and he worked 3 years at a company job while I worked 3 years for them. $10,000 was a lot of money back then and I made $10,000 and he made $20,000 and I was his direct supervisor!!" **(Jane Larson Belling)** Carroll University

"There were separate job ads and women could only be secretaries or teachers, but had to quit if they were married and pregnant. Title 9 (IX) finally required Harvard to admit women. Supreme Court Justice Sandra Day O'Connor, who was second in her law school class couldn't get hired as a lawyer, only as a legal secretary, since she was a woman. Health care plans have been able to limit what health care women receive since "men were treated equally" since they didn't get maternity or contraception birth control coverage either." **(Maura Garcia)** Bryn Mawr College

"I worked for a company in 2000 that was paying me a lower commission rate than the men were receiving. I only found it out because we talked privately about our salaries and commissions. The battle isn't over, and anyone who thinks women get paid the same as men are being naive or ignoring facts." (**Ruth Tourjee**)

"An application to work at Sears asked, "How many days of work will you miss each month because of your menstrual period?" (**Mary Kacker**) Social Work at DSHS

"In 1971 we could not wear pants to work....nor could little girls wear pants in the winter. It was strictly forbidden. In 1975 that rule was done away with." (**Elizabeth Zemia Kasprzak**) Windsor T College, 1965 U of M

"Marvelous piece so important to inform young women of women's struggle for human rights. I took it upon myself, when as a mature student, I discovered that many of the young women students weren't aware even of the progress made during the sixties. I felt it was my duty to point out that for instance maternity leave was not available when my first child was born and consequently, my job was lost! The young women were shocked as they had taken this right for granted!" (**Deirdre Houston**) IT Sligo, Ireland

"In 1980 as a newlywed in Tucson, the Sr. Partner of the CPA firm fired me as their receptionist, saying, "It has come to my attention that you are married?" "yes." "And that you are the sole source of income in that marriage?" "Yes, my husband is a Sr. finishing college at the University. He graduates this May." "Well, that's against my religion. I'm a Mormon. It's against God's will for a woman to be the sole source of income in a marriage. You'll have to pack up your things and go home. Right now." So, I had to leave, stand in the desert sun, walk in the hot desert sand in hose and heels (wasn't allowed to wear pants there either), and wait for a bus. I was too young then at 21 to know I had any rights, and went the next day to get a secretarial job at the University. I said to hell with him!" **(Jane KY Kini Malia)** Alverno College

"In addition, I am 75 years old, have gone up the management ladder and have never been discriminated against. I have never been treated as a second class citizen. If you apply yourself equally, take into consideration you have different company loyalties than a male in marriage and take more time off for these responsibilities, then don't expect to be paid the same as the male who does not have to leave the job. If I owned a business, would I want to give the femail equal pay for unequal time put into the job? No. That would be fair." **(Pat Caldwell)** Adjunct Nursing Faculty at Virgina College
S Weeks Response: "That is assuming that today's married couples share responsibilities the old way when many couples today share all responsibilities, including parenting equally."

"In 1991 I was working part-time for a local newspaper in Illinois. My male boss called me one day and said he was letting me go as he was giving my job to a man who needed it and making it full time employment. Yes, I said the year was 1991. I stand for women's rights". **(Lynn Marti Puryear)** Manpower Business Training Institute

"I hope young women read this. Thank you. In 1979 I was interviewing for a new nursing job. The HR rep asked me if

I planned to have children. When I politely reminded him, he could not ask me such a question, he sighed and said, "I guess you know your rights." I was hired then refused to sign up for "couples" healthcare. It cost so much more! My husband had coverage and I had coverage. Again I was reminded, that I "hmmm, knew my rights." We should know and continue to assert our rights. Or what has been done will be in vain. Know your rights and assert yourself when necessary." **(Margie Trosil)** Chair, Associate Professor, Div. of Nursing at Iowa Wesleyan University

Chapter IX

General Comments

Printed as received without editing.

Well said & much needed. Thank you for this. Tragic to feel like we are going backwards with white men seeming positioned to make major, negative decisions that will affect women's lives. Also want to mention a book I have not been near in a long time, "Herstory." Focuses on the contributions of women in history." **(Kathy Smith)** Utica College

"I said that to my husband when Trump was running for Pres. "Have you read the Handmaid's Tale? I see a lot of parallels. If you haven't read it, you should." **(Julie L. Hrivnak)** Bellevue College

"Well written and informative, thank you. The problem is many who will read this article are like minded, the majority who should read this will not." **(Paulette Parente Hahn)**

"This is a must article for all men and women, the power of a few in charge can change every stride made in the last 200 years. Drop your Lattes and Pilates and get involved!!!" **(Jim Sniscak)** Retired

"Every woman, man and teenager needs to see "Iron Jawed Angels." Wonderful depiction of what it took to get women the Right to Vote." **(Marianne Brodlo)** Sales at REMAX 440

"A good article. Thanks for sharing. No surprise that "The Handmaid's Tale" is now in huge demand. The seeds of this dystopia are being sown now, and it's important to stand against those who would turn the clock back". **(Jane Jenner)** McMaster University

" Men need to remember the struggle also." **(David Baker)**

"Great, you are right, every woman should and must read this." **(Tamara Suarez)** Caracas, Venezuela

"Thank you good lady." **(Russ McGillivray)** Ajijic, Jalisco, Mexico

"Thank you for this. What a great Piece!" **(Becky Epstein)** Executive Director at B'nai Havurah

"Everyone – man or woman – should read this excellent article." **(Stephen John)**

"Thank you!" **(Suzanne Rees Glanister)** London, United Kingdom

"Oh No! The sky is falling...." **(Jim McKenna)** West Chester, PA

"Awesome lady!!!" **(Paula Marsman)** Liceo de Ninas N° 1 Santiago, Chili

"YOU ALL UNDERSTAND SHE STATES FACTS GOING BACK TO 1870, NOT 1970 RIGHT???? don't be so hellbent on missing the f'ing point!" **(Sheri Bianca Wilson-Edwards)** Burbank, California

"But she persisted!!! **(Susan Sciotto-Brown)** Director, Regulatory Affairs at Profectus Biosciences, Inc.

"Sad how many STEPFORD WIVES kneeled before their masters in this past election and just bowing and serving up themselves on a platter, but serving up their daughters, too, as MINDLESSLY OBEDIENT MAIDENS of the ULTRA-WEALTHY WHITE MASTER CLASS - The Dictating Corporate Owners of the RNC and their members in Congress. HYPOCRISY is SOP in the GOP and their PARTY-OF-HATE." **(Don Sammons)** Frogmore, South Carolina

"Well written and I have to get this article in the hands of my Son and Daughters." **(Jack Kohout)** Retired

"Imagine. Again, it all boiled down to being.....white....and male!" **(Lynda Musser Belloma)** National Sales Training manager, Warner Communications NYC

"Brava!" **(Jim Reilly** (University of Minnesota)

"There is a wonderful movie that chronicles several generations of women of the same family title, "A Will of Their Own" and covers many of the issues and movements mentioned in this article. I always thought I should give copies to the next generation women in my family so they could understand women's history. Now I realize how important it is for all young women of today. The DVD is available through Amazon." **(Sally Beatty Barto)** Snoqualmie, Washington

227

"I just have to tell you Thank you. Thank you. Thank you. Every word, genius. So true...needs to be said over and over and over, until they realize our rights can be taken away (by men) at any time. We can't take them for granted. We can't close our eyes. I'm in CA and ran across this article. The best things I've read since Gloria Steinem. Thank you." **(Heide Guio)**

"What every mother should tell her daughter. Her husband. And especially her son. Sent this to my daughter and some other young ladies I know." **(Nancy Harmn)**

"Sent this to my daughter and some other young ladies I know." **(Phil Manson)** University of Georgia

"It still pervades. My son is a classical ballet dancer. When a female acquaintance learned he was taking ballet lessons when he was a child, she said, "Your husband allows you to put him in ballet class?" My husband is the person who drove him to classes most of his childhood. The word 'allows' sent a chill down my spine. This woman was a professional in her own right. This seismic pervades in large and small ways even to this day and women perpetuate it at times without knowing it." **(Val Winn)**

"I have watched many Trump gatherings over the last several painful months and have seen as many women as men vigorously supporting him. Are they blind or just stupid? Frustrating." **(Robert Smith)** Retired

"Powerful message. To all my friends and contacts: please, please read through and do whatever you can to keep American women free to be." **(Kniti Crochetoo)** Bumble Bee, AZ

"There is so much omission here that basic truths are not recognized." **(Don Turrer)** Webmaster & Facebook Admin at WNY BluesSociety

"A must read for all who have a brain." **(Scott Lowe)** Owner at Advanced Appraisal

"Our sons and grandsons need to read this." **(Ferol Bartley-Vitalis)** Taylors Falls High School

"Eau Claire Memorial class of '65, I thank you!" **(Annie Zeck)** Clinton, Washington

"Thank you Sharon Weeks, so easy to be complacent. I will now read The Handmaiden's Tale" **(Rhona Teehan)** Dublin, Ireland

"I recall seeing a comment below news article once from a Conservative who believed they were a Christian, say "So what if a woman dies from an abortion, it's God's punishment." Where does Jesus say this? And for that matter, where does Jesus say his followers have a right to judge and condemn another? What I see is that it is God who makes that call, not mankind." **(Delores Kirkwood)** Niles, Michigan

"Sounds like the current Muslim Extremists. Very interesting Nut Shell of Women's history in the USA." **(George Purvis)** Yoga Teacher at BKS Iyengar Yoga Studio of Dallas

"Only goes to show that your never content." **(Arthur Bunting)** U Mass Lowell

"Speaking of terrific, right-wing talk radio hosts, like Rush Limbaugh, have done a "terrific" job of convincing their listeners that any women out there who are still concerned about equal rights for women are Femi-nazis and by inference man-haters. Give the creep credit for coming up with a phrase that has stuck and, I believe, it helps explain why so many white college-educated women voted for Donald Trump." **(Alfred Morgan)**

"I rent "Equal Means Equal" on Amazon, which is a new documentary on the state of women's equality issues and I learned SO MUCH even as a seasoned feminist. I urge everyone to watch. Yes, you are right, we must not become complacent. We are STILL not federally protected in the Constitution. I am joining the movement to #ratifyERA now." **(Anita French)**

"It is gratifying to see women and our male supporters out marching for the programs that we have. However, and I say this out of the most respect for your article, but it doesn't matter if everyone of us doesn't vote for people and parties who support these programs. The most recent elections to fill vacant seats from Trump's cabinet and other appointments...under 20%. If you have the luxury to travel and take off work to march, you have the time to go vote. Stop voting for the same old folks, who say they support your rights, but turn around and vote the other way. Stop voting for these Red's who say they are disturbed by what Trump is saying and doesn't always support his policies, and vote for people who actually do. People who are willing to investigate, impeach, and find him guilty of endangering this country with his constant lying and his obvious ties and obligation to Russia" **(Linda Nightingale)** Emporia State University

"Should be on the bulletin board of every school and post office." **(Diana E. Long)** Yale University

"I am very afraid for my daughters, granddaughters and nieces." **(Julie Farrell)** Blenheim, Ontario, Canada

"And we lived through a lot of it. I started Nursing School in 1956 in Portsmouth, VA. Had separate delivery rooms, nurseries, OR's, ER entrances, water fountains, bathrooms, back of the bus seats, separate wards for non-whites. Also we female nurses had to stand when the male Dr.s entered the nurses' station and they sat in our chairs. We handed them the charts and practically had to curtsy. This continued for the three years I was there. I graduated in 1959 and returned to NYC. I worked at NYU. We still had to stand for those docs. The racist stuff was not as apparent, but was still there as it is today." **(Pat Phelan)**

"I am a Republican, but this summary should be seen by everyone. I am going to send this to my senators. Thank you very much. I agree 100% with everything you wrote. **(Julie Rasmussen Johnson)**

"Very Powerful article! It is so easy to fall into complacency, to think that the way things are now is the way they've always been. Yes, I'm a white male, but I know too well the struggles of the working class, the aged, and those with physical and mental challenges. We must always be ready to stand up to those who have some sick desire to oppress others." **(Michael Jarmula)** Cube Dweller at Last Remnants of American Manufacturing

231

"It's now the 21st century, wake up and live for the now, you and others are continuing to live and dwell on the past. We all know the past events happened but have chosen to live our lives in the present. Don't tell others what and how to think unless you want us to tell you how to do the same." **(Keona Kreamer)** Retired, Iowa State

"The title on my first house, purchased in 1991, gave my name, "an unmarried woman," and the rest of the information" **(Kathy Dimont)** Colorado State University

"Thank you for this extremely valuable history on women's struggles to get to where we are. I, too, am terrified the direction our present government is going." **(Barb Nicholson)** Program Assistant at State of Wisconsin

"OMG WOMEN!!! PLEASE READ<><>" **(Marsha Coutu)** Natrona County High School, Casper, WY

"I am 79 years old. When I was divorced in 1970, I was unable to rent an apartment because I had two kids, but no husband. I was refused a credit card. I remarried the man. I remember I needed a car, I was refused credit unless he signed for it. I was working full time! I worked for 30 years for national companies who paid me a little over half what the men were paid, for doing the same work. I was young and attractive, I had to listen to sly sexual innuendo by fellow male workers and top bosses. No......these young women have no idea what it was like." **(Kathy Haas Nash)** West Falls, NY

"Even if you do not agree with these facts, all girls and women must be aware of all this history. This was important to my mother and her 3 sisters in the 20's, 30's and

40's. It has been important to me and friends, families ever since the 1950's to the present. We do not have to agree, but the facts and history are very important to know and remember !!" **(Mareda Peters)** University of Texas at Dallas

"Ken Burns' "Not for Ourselves Alone" is a terrific movie on the women's rights movement. All Americans should see it. Point to ponder......Even our movement for equality is told by men......"**(Lyn Des Marais)** Legislative Director at Vermont   Farm   Bureau **Respons**e **Sharon Weeks**: Thank you for that, will get the movie.

"My daughter just had me read Margaret Atwood's "Handmaid's Tale". I found it to be deeply disturbing. The way things are being allowed to happen within our government currently could make this prophetic is more terrifying. It's easy to be in denial and think that it couldn't happen, but are you sure? One by one rights and privileges can be removed and some may not notice it at all until it's just too late." **(Penny Wied Navrestad)**

"The Night of Terror", 11-15-1917. See HBO movie "Iron Jawed Angels."

"As a man I am ashamed. Eye opener." **(Jim Jd Ditton)**

"The disparity among the women who have either had a difficult time establishing credit for all the wrong reasons and those who had an easier time begs the question of why? Why did some have a harder time than others? What differences were there in the areas, the lifestyles, that made such a difference?" **(Holly Manheim)**

S Weeks Response: "Just reading over 4,000 responses. I can tell you a lot of it had to do with where they lived and whether a small town or city."

"In this essagy lies the fatal flaw that will conitnue to plague our country. Ms. Weeks is referring to white women as satisfied with "status quo" of their lives. Young women of color do not feel that was at all. As a retired teacher, her referencing that blacks received citizenship and suffrage through the 14th & 15th Amendments is appalling when there is no mention of 1964 Voting Rights Act, which finally allowed black Americans to excercise that rifhts granted by those amendments on the basi elements. I found this piece and classic example of the arrogance and ignorance of most well meaning European Maerican women when it comes to equity. If equlity only matters when they are personally being effected, and any other group impacted only gets to play a bit part. By far, European American woemn have benefited the most of any other group from the Civil Rights movement in the 1960's....yet, they are the onles who are raising the complacent young women. They are as so the ones that sit in most human resource departments and set compensation policies. So, next time.... please be clear one who needs to wake up and join the entire fight for Life, Liberty & the Pursuit of Happiness in Am"erica." **(Dan Stephenson)**

S Weeks Response: "Maybe you missed the title, "What Young Women MAY not Know". The "status quo" was aimed at the young women who think marchers are whiners and that everything in their life is perfect. The point was to

234

learn something from history. A perfect life now, if you have one, is wonderful, but know why it is wonderful and how easily it can be lost. Throughout history groups of people have marched for many different reasons and people who are not aware of these things in the past need to know about it. Thus the reason for including marches for many reasons was made to show their importance, but the article was strictly about women's rights. Newspapers have limits on the length of articles, but it wasn't my intent to cover everyone and everything. (...and I am not a retired teacher.)"

"Great piece by Margaret Atwood in recent NY Times about "Handmaids Tale" in the age of Trump if you haven't seen it. **(John Porcher)** Insect Trapper at State of Utah

"It was my privilege to have met Ms. Weeks and photographed her at the East End Fringe Festivals''s "The Future is Female" on 3-23-17 when she traveled to Riverhead, NY.(regarding her article What Young Women May Not Know) Her presence is sparkling."[32]. **(Miranda Gatewood)** Miranda Gatewood Photography **S Weeks Response:** "Thank you Miranda. It was a privilege to meet you and to see your wonderful photography. About Miranda Gatewood.[33] She holds an M.F.A. in fine art photography from the Cranbrook Academy of Art, Bloomfield Hills, MI and enjoyed a 12-year tenure as editor of Networking magazine, a women's business monthly. Miranda Gatewood is available for portraiture, event photography and fine art commissions."

"BBC "Ascent of Woman" is an excellent watch." **(Rachel Ovens)** Registered Nurse at Little Sisters of the Poor

"I learned my Great grandma Otillie Suits was from LAC Du Flambeau Indian tribe half Chippewa. She lived in Medford, Wi. Since she married a doctor, I believe her life was less as "property" and more as helpmate. My Grandpa lived his entire life in Medford and my Dad moved there to take over family drugstore when I was a teenager. My Grandma was a stay at home Mom, but she had her own opinions so I feel blessed when my own Mom, who graduated from Milwaukee Downer College, brought me up to be tolerant, to not believe in a glass ceiling and I believe my own daughters also feel that way and I believe my granddaughters will also be brought up to have good values. Good article." **(Karen Jackie)** California State University, Long Beach

"One of the texts I use in my women's lit class in Bangledesh is The Handmaid's Tale; my students are always shocked as to how relevant it is to life here today...and possibly to the near future scenario in the US." **(Razia Sultana Khan)** University of Nebraska – Lincoln

"I couldn't have said it better." **(April Lee Moore Washburn)** Lake Superior State College 1975-1982

"Thank you for that information. I learned a lot." **(Terry M. McGrane)** Machinist at John Deere

"Excellent summary of the long fought war for equality in every phase of our lives." **(Paulette Kevin)** Maryville University

"In the early 70's when I was purchasing an outfit for work I was asked if I wanted to open an account. I had never had credit in my own name, it was always Mr. & Mrs. We had excellent credit and I was denied. When we bought our home I made substantially more, but I was listed last. I was a parts manager for a large wholesale company. I was told many times by walk-in customers, "I want to see a man" or "I never thought I'd see a woman in a hardware store." I can't imagine what it was like for my mother and grandmother." **(Gwen Kelly)** Washington State University

"The Girls of Atomic City by Denise Kiernan, the untold story of the women who helped win World War II, A great read!" **(Sharon Weeks)**

"Margaret Atwood lived in Berlin with the Wall. She KNOWS how quickly things change...a matter of weeks or months...and it's all changed. **"(Jo Scherer)** Indianola, Washington

"The Handmaids Tale scared me to death. The ancient Irish in prehistory looked at women as equals. They had their own property which their spouse could not touch. They had all rights women today have to fight tooth and nail just to get a nibble of these days & we are all aware those old, white men want to take it all away & will kill to do it". **(Gail Arseneau)**

"Women position is one of adults when US spread democracy with bombs in East. US have a lot of work to implement democracy on own territory. No time for other countries, despite reward in control of other (mostly east) countries and oil." **(Perla Grass)** Tehnicki skolski centar Ruder Boskovic

"When I read "Handmaid's Tale" many years ago, I thought that it could never happen in the 20th century, especially not in the US. I also thought Donald Trump was amusing, but no one with any sense would vote for him. I don't want to draw to close a comparison, but until recently, I didn't understand how so many people could be drawn in by Hitler" **(Virginia Veileca)** Atlanta, Georgia

"What a load of propaganda by Feminists who have made women's lives more exhausting than ever!" **(Carmel Jennings)** Ticket Wear, self employed contractor

"Reading   If This Goes On, a science fiction novella by American writer Robert A. Heinlein`" **(Terry Miller)** Skyline High School, Idaho

"Great article.   Just a small correction, in the final paragraph, the spelling should be "complaisant. **(Kimberly Dijkstra)**   Anton   Media   Group **S Weeks Response**:   "Actually, it isn't wrong.   It is "complacent"."

"You rock Sharon - proud to be part of the same gallery." **(Flossie Irvine)** Chippewa Falls, WI

"I'm just a guy!! But I stand with you all!!" **(George Davis)** Propmaker   at   Latse   Local   44 **Response**: **Stacy Marie** Delete "just"?

"Chills run down my back at what we could lose in 4 years or less. We must RESIST". **(Darla Trapp)** CFO at NAMI San Diago

"Mexicans are as diverse as the stars. Most Mexicans in "American" are US citizens. Most Mexicans are not in fear of having family members deported. Most Mexicans in Mexico don't view Americans as having much understanding regarding their own American history. Most Mexicans in Mexico know they are American, and equally North American. Most Mexicans in the USA and in the United States of Mexico never immigrated, they were already here. Most Mexicans can trace their ancestry to centuries prior to the arrival of most European Americans in the 1800's." **(Nico Genova)**

"Thanxs so much Stephanie! We are Powerful women! That's all that matters" **(Irene Brendah Tamale)** Makerere University, Uganda

"Yes. Complacency is the breeding ground for tyranny." **(Jo Noi)** Michigan State University

"It is not just an American summary - it corresponds to many countries at the same times. The sixties brought about many political changes for women across the world, but it is true that these freedoms are being changed and reversed as we speak. **(Cynthia Prentice)**

"Just wanted you to know that this wonderful piece was shared on Facebook by a friend of mine in the Seattle area. EC is my hometown! Thank you to you and all the strong women who went before." **(Suzanne Perkins)**

"This information should go viral for every woman in the world. No, we shouldn't become complacent at all. Our daughters, granddaughters and the future generation of women need this info. Make a copy for your household to read.....as a discussion." **(Irma Ramirez Rangel)**

"I wish both my granddaughters would read this, but they have disconnected from me over the election. I do not know how to reach them anymore. This is a great article, very well-written. Thanks for sharing." **(Lindell Stacy-Horton)**

*Well said." **(Gene Thompson)** Minneapolis, MN

"I am not a woman, but I am all in, supporting your efforts to educate everyone as to how we got here, and why we must continue going forward, never backward..It's not just a woman's issue, it's a human rights issue." **(Richard Sweeney)** Northwestern University Dental School

"I was just reading this thread - the bar is SO LOW that women are thanking men for supporting the equality of women and praising them for not feeling threatened and insecure. "Thank you for equal pay" - "Thank you for letting me vote" - "Thank you for allowing me to have reproductive choice" - This isn't about asking permission. This isn't about "once upon a time". I didn't have access to a library card. There are real threats facing women - just like you may have faced - happening now in 2017". **(Stacy Marie)**

"Veldig god paminnelse!" **(Britt Stene)** Norway

"Sending to my God daughter's sorority. Well done indeed." **(Bonnie Barclay)** Norcross, Georgia

"Excellent column!" **(Megal Hollbrook)** CEO/Found/Owner at Digitalese LLC

"This is a brief and entirely tue synopsis of what woman have gone through and had to endure of many years of history! All I ask you do do - as a female in this country - is to be informed. If you can read this history and walk away unconcerned and undedicated to do whatever you can to make the lives of women in the united states BETTER, then we do not have anything in common beyond what we were given a birth, our sexuality. Have a good life!" **(Sue Weinheimer)** Seattle, Washington

"All women should be aware of their history......we are still rated second class; when in actuality we are first class. Sobering facts." **(Linda Brown)** Liverpool, Nova Scotia

"It's oh so easy to feel "lucky" that women have "never had it so good." No, not lucky. It was a hard won fight." **(Dawn May)** Keel University, Staffordshire, United Kingdom

"Absolutely understand the importance of this historical struggle and remember it. Stay alert - all can be reversed."**(Catherine Hammond)** Perth, Western Australia

"Thank you for a reminder of women's history." **(Tytti Lanford)** Helsingin yliopisto, Finland

Chapter X

Recommended by Readers

MOVIES, VIDEOS, READING RECOMMENDED BY OTHER READERS

*Not For Ourselves Alone | Home | Ken Burns DVDs https://www.pbs.org/kenburns/not-for-ourselves-alone The Story of **Elizabeth Cady Stanton & Susan B**. Anthony: Not For Ourselves Alone is a co-production of Florentine Films and WETA. Corporate underwriting provided by: Additional underwriting ..

The Patrons of Husbandry | Tennessee Encyclopedia https://tennesseeencyclopedia.net/entries/the-patrons-of-husbandry Oct 08, 2017 · The Patrons of Husbandry, or Grange, was the **first general farm organization in the United States**. Established by the Minnesota agricultural reformer Oliver H. Kelly in December 1867, it briefly flourished in Tennessee during the 1870s, providing Tennessee's small farmers with opportunities for economic, political, and social expression.

No Constitutional Right to Be Ladies: Kerber, Linda ... https://www.amazon.com/Constitutional-Right-Ladies...Sep 01, 1999 · An original and compelling consideration of

American **law** and culture, **No Constitutional Right to Be Ladies** emphasizes the dangers of excluding women from other civic responsibilities as well, such as loyalty oaths and jury duty. Exploring the lives of the plaintiffs, the strategies of the lawyers, and the decisions of the courts, Kerber offers readers a convincing argument for equal treatment under the **Cited by:** 387 **Author:** Linda K. Kerber   Site lists the book.

A Will of Their Own (TV Mini-Series 1998) - IMDb
https://www.imdb.com/title/tt0149441*Oct 18, 1998* · With Eric McCormack, Paris Jefferson, David New, Karin Anglin. A two-part epic that "chronicles women's lives in the 20th century"

Amazon.com: Watch Equal Means Equal | Prime Video
https://www.amazon.com/Equal-Means-Patricia-Arquette/dp/B01LG6H17Q Equal Means Equal. (48) IMDb 6.2 1h 33min 2016 NR. EQUAL MEANS EQUAL is a **groundbreaking exploration of gender inequality in the USA featuring top women's rights activists and leaders**. A brutal expose of a broken system, the film reignites the dialogue on full equality for all Americans. There are several websites for Equal Means Equal

Amazon.com: Maafa 21: Black Genocide In 21st Century
https://www.amazon.com/Maafa-21-Genocide-Century-America/dp/B003I5I6DE
This is a documentary that outlines a number of ways in

which slavery continues into the 21st-century. This is an important piece of history regarding eugenics.

Phyllis Schlafly - Wikipedia

https://en.wikipedia.org/wiki/Phyllis_Schlafly Phyllis Stewart Schlafly was a movement conservative and author. She held conservative social and political views, opposed feminism and abortion, and successfully campaigned against ratification of the Equal Rights Amendment to the U.S. Constitution

A website search will bring up multiple listings for Phyllis Schlafly including her history and also books she had written.

Stage Coach Mary | Historic Path of Cattaraugus County

historicpath.com/article/stage-coach-mary-841 Stage Coach Mary was born into **slavery in TN** and named **Mary Fields**. Her slave master was a Judge. Mary was a 6 ft, 250lb woman who knew how to shoot, carried a pistol and rifle on her at all times, drank whiskey, smoked cigars, didn't take shit from anyone, and was extremely hard working, loyal and intelligent

Good and Mad: The Revolutionary Power of Women's Anger ...

https://www.amazon.com/Good-Mad-Revolutionary...Oct 02, 2018 · "**Good and Mad** is Rebecca Traister's ode to women's rage—an extensively researched history and analysis of its political power. It is a thoughtful, granular examination: Traister considers how perception (and tolerance) of women's anger shifts based on which women hold it (*cough* white women *cough*) and who they direct it toward; she points to the ways in which women are shamed for or …

https://www.cracked.com/article_23128_5-remarkable-women-who-got-totally-screwed-out-history.html
A website that deserves a look!

Iron Jawed Angels - Wikipedia
https://en.wikipedia.org/wiki/Iron_Jawed_Angels
Iron Jawed Angels is a 2004 American historical drama film directed by Katja von Garnier. The film stars Hilary Swank as suffragist leader Alice Paul, Frances O'Connor as activist Lucy Burns, Julia Ormond as Inez Milholland, and Anjelica Huston as Carrie Chapman Catt. It received critical acclaim after the film premiered at the 2004 Sundance Film Festival. The film focuses on the American women's suffragemovement during the 1910s and follows women's s…

The Girls of Atomic City: The Untold Story of the Women ...
https://www.goodreads.com/book/show/15801668-the-girls-of-atomic-city
This is the perfectly executed history book: It tells a story from a side (women) that most people haven't heard. It includes female scientists, African American women, native Tennessee women, transplants from the city, transplants from the prairie, and interactions between the women and

Japanese women years immediately –and years- after the bomb fell.   S Week: An excellent read!

The Girls Who Went Away: The Hidden History of Women Who ...
https://www.amazon.com/Girls-Who-Went-Away-Surrendered/dp/0143038974 Jun 26, 2007 · The Girls Who Went Away, a book by A. Fessler (2006)

Mercury 13 - Wikipedia
https://en.wikipedia.org/wiki/Mercury_13 The Mercury 13 were thirteen American women who, as part of a privately funded program, successfully underwent the same physiological screening tests as had the astronauts selected by NASA on April 9, 1959 for Project Mercury.

The Handmaid's Tale - Wikipedia
https://en.wikipedia.org/wiki/The_Handmaid's_Tale
The Handmaid's Tale is a dystopian novel by Canadian author Margaret Atwood, published in 1985. It is set in a near-future New England, in a totalitarian state, known as Gilead, that has overthrown the United States government. The Handmaid's Tale explores themes of subjugated women in a patriarchal society and the various means by which these women resist and attempt to gain individuality and independence **S Weeks**: A must read and a must watch (the TV series on Hulu)!

Where are they from............

N ot everyone left their name, and not everyone left their location, but 1,087 people left at least a city, state, province or country.

The vastness of the article's reach blew me away!

Kings Meadows	Tasmania	Australia
Appolo Bay	Victoria	Australia
Clayton	Victoria	Australia
	Victoria	Australia
Northcote	Victoria	Australia
Perth	Western Australia	Australia
Airdrie	Alberta	Canada
Calgary	Alberta	Canada
Mallacoota	Alberta	Canada
Chestermere	Alberta	Canada
Chestermere	Alberta	Canada
Edmonton	Alberta	Canada
Edmonton	Alberta	Canada
	Alberta	Canada
	Alberta	Canada
	Alberta	Canada
Richmond	British Columba	Canada
Burnaby	British Columbia	Canada
Burnaby	British Columbia	Canada
Burnaby	British Columbia	Canada
Delta	British Columbia	Canada
Fraser Valley	British Columbia	Canada

Langley	British Columbia	Canada
Langley	British Columbia	Canada
Nelson	British Columbia	Canada
New Westminster	British Columbia	Canada
Victoria	British Columbia	Canada
	British Columbia	Canada
Vancouver	British Columbia	Canada
St. John's	Newfoundland & Labrador	Canada
	Newfoundland & Labrador	Canada
Liverpool	Nova Scotia	Canada
Antigonish	Nova Scotia	Canada
Blenheim	Ontario	Canada
Cobourg	Ontario	Canada
Cobourg	Ontario	Canada
Hamilton	Ontario	Canada
London	Ontario	Canada
Niagara Falls	Ontario	Canada
North York	Ontario	Canada
Oakville	Ontario	Canada
Oakville	Ontario	Canada
Oshawa	Ontario	Canada
Ottawa	Ontario	Canada

Ottawa	Ontario	Canada
Richmond Hill	Ontario	Canada
Thunder Bay	Ontario	Canada
Toronto	Ontario	Canada
Toronto	Ontario	Canada
	Ontario	Canada
	Ontario	Canada
Montreal	Quebec	Canada
Montreal	Quebec	Canada
Montreal	Quebec	Canada
Montreal	Quebec	Canada
Regina	Saskatchewan	Canada
Saskatoon	Saskatchewan	Canada
White Horse	Yukon	Canada
Santiago		Chile
Jastrebarsko		Croatia
Ruder Boskovic		Croatia
Helsinki		Finland
Paris		France
Muenchen		Germany
Dublin		Ireland
Beitar Illit		Israel
Matera		Italy

Ajlgic		Jalisco	Mexico
			Mexico
Nuenen			Netherlands
			Norway
Coimbra			Portugal
Abu Dhabi			Saudi Arabia
Jeddah			Saudi Arabia
Riyadh			Saudi Arabia
Edinburgh			Scotland
Valencia			Spain
Port of Spain			Trinidad & Tobago
Kampala			Uganda
Keel		New Castle	UK
Liverpool			UK
London			UK
London			UK
Peterborough			UK
			UK
Abu Dhabi			United Arab Emirates
San Juan		Puerto Rico	USA
Sagrado Corazon	Santruce	Puerto Rico	USA
Boston	MA		USA
Tucson	AZ		USA

Anchorage	AK	USA
Anchorage	AK	USA
Kodiak Island	AK	USA
Huntsville	AL	USA
Scottsboro	AL	USA
Fort Smith	AR	USA
Hot Springs	AR	USA
Hot Springs National Park	AR	USA
Little Rock	AR	USA
Little Rock	AR	USA
Oden	AR	USA
Tucson	AR	USA
Bumble Bee	AZ	USA
Burbank	AZ	USA
Mesa	AZ	USA
Phoenix	AZ	USA
Phoenix	AZ	USA
Phoenix	AZ	USA
Phoenix	AZ	USA
Phoenix	AZ	USA
Prescott	AZ	USA
Sun City	AZ	USA
Tucson	AZ	USA

Yuma	AZ	USA
Aptos	CA	USA
Aptos	CA	USA
Arcata	CA	USA
Atherton	CA	USA
Banning	CA	USA
Bella Vista	CA	USA
Berkeley	CA	USA
Berkeley	CA	USA
Berkeley	CA	USA
Berkley	CA	USA
Campbell	CA	USA
Campbell	CA	USA
Carlsbad	CA	USA
Chico	CA	USA
Claremont	CA	USA
Covina	CA	USA
Culver City	CA	USA
Cupertino	CA	USA
Daly City	CA	USA
Dana Point	CA	USA
Davis	CA	USA
El Dorado Hills	CA	USA

Eureka	CA	USA
Fair Oaks	CA	USA
Fresno	CA	USA
Grass Valley	CA	USA
Kentfield	CA	USA
La Habra	CA	USA
La Jolla	CA	USA
La Palma	CA	USA
Laguna Niguel	CA	USA
Lake Oroville	CA	USA
Long Beach	CA	USA
Long Beach	CA	USA
Long Beach	CA	USA
Long Beach	CA	USA
Los Angeles	CA	USA
Los Angeles	CA	USA
Los Angeles	CA	USA
Los Angeles	CA	USA
Los Angeles	CA	USA
Los Angles	CA	USA
Modesto	CA	USA
Modesto	CA	USA
Monterey Park	CA	USA

Morgan Hills	CA	USA
Napa Valley	CA	USA
Napa Valley	CA	USA
North Ridge	CA	USA
Oakdale	CA	USA
Palm Desert	CA	USA
Palo Alto	CA	USA
Paramount	CA	USA
Pasadena	CA	USA
Playa del Rey	CA	USA
Pomona	CA	USA
Pomona	CA	USA
Pomona	CA	USA
Redding	CA	USA
Redlands	CA	USA
Ridgecrest	CA	USA
Ridgecrest	CA	USA
Sacramento	CA	USA
Sacramento	CA	USA
Sacramento	CA	USA
San Bernardino	CA	USA
San Bernardino	CA	USA
San Bernardino	CA	USA

San Bernardino	CA	USA
San Diego	CA	USA
San Diego	CA	USA
San Francisco	CA	USA
San Francisco	CA	USA
San Francisco	CA	USA
San Francisco	CA	USA
San Francisco	CA	USA
San Francisco	CA	USA
San Francisco	CA	USA
San Jose	CA	USA
San Jose	CA	USA
San Jose	CA	USA
San Jose	CA	USA
San Jose	CA	USA
San Luis Obispo	CA	USA
Santa Barbers	CA	USA
Santa Cruz	CA	USA
Santa Cruz	CA	USA
Santa Monica	CA	USA
Santa Monica	CA	USA
Santa Monica	CA	USA
Santa Rosa	CA	USA

Santa Rosa	CA	USA
Santa Rosa	CA	USA
Stanford	CA	USA
Stanford	CA	USA
Stanford	CA	USA
Stanford	CA	USA
Stockton	CA	USA
Stockton	CA	USA
Summerville	CA	USA
Sunnyvale	CA	USA
Vacaville	CA	USA
Valencia	CA	USA
Ventura	CA	USA
Weimar	CA	USA
Westwood	CA	USA
Whittier	CA	USA
Yucca Valley	CA	USA
Boulder	CO	USA
Boulder	CO	USA
Boulder	CO	USA
Delta	CO	USA
Denver	CO	USA
Denver	CO	USA

Denver	CO	USA
Denver	CO	USA
Denver	CO	USA
Fort Collins	CO	USA
Fort Collins	CO	USA
Longmont	CO	USA
Westminster	CO	USA
Danbury	CT	USA
Hartford	CT	USA
Hartford	CT	USA
New Haven	CT	USA
New Haven	CT	USA
New Haven	CT	USA
New Haven	CT	USA
New Haven	CT	USA
New London	CT	USA
Putnam	CT	USA
Simsbury	CT	USA
Storrs	CT	USA
Storrs	CT	USA
Trumbull	CT	USA
Uncasville	CT	USA
West Haven	CT	USA

Westbury	CT	USA
Woodstock	CT	USA
Washington	DC	USA
Washington	DC	USA
Washington	DC	USA
Washington	DC	USA
Washington	DC	USA
Newark	DE	USA
Newark	DE	USA
Newark	DE	USA
Boynton Beach	FL	USA
Boynton Beach	FL	USA
Deerfield Beach	FL	USA
Fort Lauderdale	FL	USA
Fort Lauderdale	FL	USA
Gainesville	FL	USA
Gainesville	FL	USA
Hollywood	FL	USA
Hollywood	FL	USA
Lakeland	FL	USA
Lakeland	FL	USA
Lighthouse Point	FL	USA
Marion County	FL	USA

Miami	FL	USA
Miami	FL	USA
Miami	FL	USA
Miami Beach	FL	USA
Mount Dora	FL	USA
New Port Richey	FL	USA
Palm Beach Gardens	FL	USA
Palm Harbor	FL	USA
Sanford	FL	USA
Sarasota	FL	USA
Seaside	FL	USA
St. Petersburg	FL	USA
St. Petersburg	FL	USA
Sunrise	FL	USA
Sunrise City	FL	USA
Tampa	FL	USA
Temple Terrace	FL	USA
Treasure Island	FL	USA
Volusia County	FL	USA
Weeki Wachee	FL	USA
West Melbourne	FL	USA
	FL	USA

Athens	GA	USA
Athens	GA	USA
Athens	GA	USA
Athens	GA	USA
Atlanta	GA	USA
Atlanta	GA	USA
Atlanta	GA	USA
Atlanta	GA	USA
Atlanta	GA	USA
Augusta	GA	USA
Cordele	GA	USA
Dahlonega	GA	USA
Decatur	GA	USA
Woodstock	GA	USA
Lahaina	HI	USA
Waimea	HI	USA
Waimea County	HI	USA
Davenport	IA	USA
Algona	IA	USA
Cedar Falls	IA	USA
Decorah	IA	USA
Dubuque	IA	USA
Huxley	IA	USA

Iowa City	IA	USA
Monroe	IA	USA
Monroe	IA	USA
Mt. Pleasant	IA	USA
Mt. Vernon	IA	USA
New Hampton	IA	USA
Ogden	IA	USA
Bonners Ferry	ID	USA
Bonners Ferry	ID	USA
Idaho Falls	ID	USA
Idaho Falls	ID	USA
Moscow	ID	USA
Moscow	ID	USA
Batavia	IL	USA
Champaign	IL	USA
Champaign	IL	USA
Chicago	IL	USA
Chicago	IL	USA
Chicago	IL	USA
Chicago	IL	USA
Chicago	IL	USA
Chicago	IL	USA
Chicago	IL	USA

Chicago	IL	USA
Chicago	IL	USA
Chicago	IL	USA
Chicago	IL	USA
Chicago	IL	USA
Chicago	IL	USA
Chicago	IL	USA
Chicago	IL	USA
Chicago	IL	USA
Chicago	IL	USA
Crystal Lake	IL	USA
Crystal Lake	IL	USA
Downers Gove	IL	USA
Evanston	IL	USA
Glen Ellyn	IL	USA
Livonia	IL	USA
Macomb	IL	USA
Macomb	IL	USA
Macomb	IL	USA
Macomb	IL	USA
Macomb	IL	USA
Mattoon	IL	USA
New Berlin	IL	USA

New Berlin	IL	USA
New Berlin	IL	USA
Normal	IL	USA
Norridge	IL	USA
Oak Park	IL	USA
Peoria	IL	USA
Peoria	IL	USA
Rockford	IL	USA
Rockford	IL	USA
Waukegan	IL	USA
Wilmette	IL	USA
Bloomington	IN	USA
Brownsburg	IN	USA
Brownsburg	IN	USA
Elkhart	IN	USA
Indianapolis	IN	USA
Indianapolis	IN	USA
Indianapolis	IN	USA
Indianapolis	IN	USA
Indianapolis	IN	USA
Lafayette	IN	USA
Lafayette	IN	USA
Muncie	IN	USA

Notre Dame	IN	USA
Vincennes	IN	USA
Vincennes	IN	USA
W. La Fayette	IN	USA
Aberdeen	IO	USA
Cedar Falls	IO	USA
Cedar Falls	IO	USA
Cedar Rapids	IO	USA
Cedar Rapids	IO	USA
Davenport	IO	USA
Davenport	IO	USA
Humeston	IO	USA
Rock Rapids	IO	USA
Concordia	KS	USA
Emporia	KS	USA
Iola	KS	USA
Kansas City	KS	USA
Lawrence	KS	USA
Lawrence	KS	USA
Lawrence	KS	USA
Manhattan	KS	USA
Ottawa	KS	USA
Pittsburg	KS	USA

Pittsburg	KS	USA
Shawnee Mission	KS	USA
Ulysses	KS	USA
West Wichita	KS	USA
West Wichita	KS	USA
Wichita	KS	USA
Winfield	KS	USA
Murray	KT	USA
Bowling Green	KY	USA
Danville	KY	USA
Florence	KY	USA
Henderson	KY	USA
Lexington	KY	USA
Louisville	KY	USA
Louisville	KY	USA
Louisville	KY	USA
Louisville	KY	USA
Louisville	KY	USA
Meta	KY	USA
Murray	KY	USA
Lafayette	LA	USA
Natchitoches	LA	USA
New Orleans	LA	USA

Schriever	LA	USA
Amherst	MA	USA
Amherst	MA	USA
Belmont	MA	USA
Beverly	MA	USA
Beverly	MA	USA
Boston	MA	USA
Boston	MA	USA
Boston	MA	USA
Boston	MA	USA
Boston	MA	USA
Boston	MA	USA
Boston	MA	USA
Boston	MA	USA
Boston	MA	USA
Boston	MA	USA
Boston	MA	USA
Boston	MA	USA
Boston	MA	USA
Boston	MA	USA
Boston	MA	USA
Brewster	MA	USA
Bridgewater	MA	USA

Brockton	MA	USA
Cambridge	MA	USA
Cambridge	MA	USA
Carlisle	MA	USA
Chestnut Hill	MA	USA
Danvers	MA	USA
Framingham	MA	USA
Framingham	MA	USA
Garner	MA	USA
Hudson	MA	USA
Leominster	MA	USA
Lowell	MA	USA
Manchester	MA	USA
Medway	MA	USA
Milton	MA	USA
Milton	MA	USA
Newton	MA	USA
Northampton	MA	USA
Pittsfield	MA	USA
Pittsfield	MA	USA
Springfield	MA	USA
West Barnstable	MA	USA
Worcester	MA	USA

Annapolis	MD	USA
Baltimore	MD	USA
Baltimore	MD	USA
Baltimore	MD	USA
Baltimore	MD	USA
Baltimore	MD	USA
Bel Air	MD	USA
Bel Air	MD	USA
Bethesda	MD	USA
College Park	MD	USA
Ellicott	MD	USA
Ellicott City	MD	USA
Hurlock	MD	USA
Laytonville	MD	USA
Notre Dame	MD	USA
Rockville	MD	USA
Rockville	MD	USA
Towson	MD	USA
Towson	MD	USA
Williamsport	MD	USA
Allendale	ME	USA
Cambridge	ME	USA
Kennebunkport	ME	USA

Mapleton	ME	USA
Orono	ME	USA
Standish	ME	USA
Ann Arbor	MI	USA
Ann Arbor	MI	USA
Ann Arbor	MI	USA
Big Rapids	MI	USA
Dearborn	MI	USA
Detroit	MI	USA
Detroit	MI	USA
Detroit	MI	USA
East Lansing	MI	USA
East Lansing	MI	USA
East Lansing	MI	USA
East Lansing	MI	USA
East Lansing	MI	USA
Fraser	MI	USA
Grand Rapids	MI	USA
Grand Rapids	MI	USA
Hancock	MI	USA
Hancock	MI	USA
Holland	MI	USA
Holland	MI	USA

Jackson	MI	USA
Kalamazoo	MI	USA
Kalamazoo	MI	USA
Kalamazoo	MI	USA
Kalamazoo	MI	USA
Lansing	MI	USA
Livonia	MI	USA
Livonia	MI	USA
Lupton	MI	USA
Marquette	MI	USA
Marquette	MI	USA
Mt. Pleasant	MI	USA
Mt. Pleasant	MI	USA
Niles	MI	USA
Rockford	MI	USA
Rockford	MI	USA
Southfield	MI	USA
St. Louis	MI	USA
Troy	MI	USA
Waterford	MI	USA
Waterford	MI	USA
Waterford	MI	USA
Ypsilanti	MI	USA

Ypsilanti	MI	USA
Zeeland	MI	USA
	MI	USA
Anoka-Ramsey	MN	USA
Burnsville	MN	USA
Collegeville	MN	USA
Collegeville	MN	USA
Collegeville	MN	USA
Coon Rapids	MN	USA
Duluth	MN	USA
Duluth	MN	USA
Duluth	MN	USA
Duluth	MN	USA
Duluth	MN	USA
Duluth	MN	USA
Ely	MN	USA
Faribault	MN	USA
Lake Elmo	MN	USA
Lake Elmo	MN	USA
Maplewood	MN	USA
Minneapolis	MN	USA
Minneapolis	MN	USA
Minneapolis	MN	USA

Minneapolis	MN	USA
Minneapolis	MN	USA
Minneapolis	MN	USA
Minneapolis	MN	USA
Minneapolis	MN	USA
Minneapolis	MN	USA
Minneapolis	MN	USA
Minneapolis	MN	USA
Minneapolis	MN	USA
Minneapolis	MN	USA
Minneapolis	MN	USA
Montgomery	MN	USA
Moorhead	MN	USA
Moorhead	MN	USA
Ogilvie	MN	USA
Prior Lake	MN	USA
Prior Lake	MN	USA
Red Wing	MN	USA
Rochester	MN	USA
Rochester	MN	USA
Rochester	MN	USA
Rochester	MN	USA
Roseville	MN	USA

Roseville	MN	USA
Sebeka	MN	USA
St. Paul	MN	USA
St. Paul	MN	USA
St. Paul	MN	USA
Taylors Falls	MN	USA
Three Oaks	MN	USA
Charles	MO	USA
Columbia	MO	USA
Gladstone	MO	USA
Grandview	MO	USA
Kansas City	MO	USA
Kansas City	MO	USA
Kirksville	MO	USA
Kirksville	MO	USA
Kirksville	MO	USA
Nevada	MO	USA
St. Louis	MO	USA
St. Louis	MO	USA
St. Louis	MO	USA
St. Louis	MO	USA
St. Peter	MO	USA
St. Peter's	MO	USA

Stephens	MO		USA
Webster Groves	MO		USA
Wentzville	MO		USA
Beverly	MS		USA
Auburn Hills	MT		USA
Billings	MT		USA
Great Falls	MT		USA
Great Falls	MT		USA
Great Falls	MT		USA
Helena	MT		USA
Livingston	MT		USA
Poplar	MT		USA
Roundup	MT		USA
San Joaquin	MT		USA
	MT		USA
Baltimore	MD		USA
Chapel Hill	NC		USA
Chapel Hill	NC		USA
Chapel Hill	NC		USA
Chapel Hill	NC		USA
Chapel Hill	NC		USA
Charleston	NC		USA
Durham	NC		USA

Durham	NC	USA
Greensboro	NC	USA
Greensboro	NC	USA
Hendersonville	NC	USA
Kernersville	NC	USA
Roanoke Rapids	NC	USA
Salisbury	NC	USA
Wilmington	NC	USA
Wilmington	NC	USA
Wilmington	NC	USA
Winston-Salem	NC	USA
Yanceyville	NC	USA
Grand Forks	ND	USA
Minnewaukan	ND	USA
Deerfield	NE	USA
Lincoln	NE	USA
Lincoln	NE	USA
Lincoln	NE	USA
	NE	USA
Belmont	NH	USA
Berlin	NH	USA
Chatham	NH	USA
Durham	NH	USA

Durham	NH	USA
Goffstown	NH	USA
Manchester	NH	USA
Manchester	NH	USA
Manchester	NH	USA
Plymouth	NH	USA
Princeton	NH	USA
Wolfeboro	NH	USA
Asbury Park	NJ	USA
Cape May	NJ	USA
Cape May	NJ	USA
Edison	NJ	USA
Jersey Shore	NJ	USA
Lawrenceville	NJ	USA
Little Fairy	NJ	USA
Marlton	NJ	USA
Millburn	NJ	USA
Millburn	NJ	USA
Mount Laurel	NJ	USA
New Brunswick	NJ	USA
New Brunswick	NJ	USA
Newark	NJ	USA
North Bergen	NJ	USA

Old Bridge	NJ	USA
Scotch Plains	NJ	USA
Smithville	NJ	USA
Toms River	NJ	USA
Trenton	NJ	USA
Wayne	NJ	USA
Weehawken	NJ	USA
Weehawken	NJ	USA
Carlsbad	NM	USA
Eunice	NM	USA
Las Cruces	NM	USA
Portales	NM	USA
Boulder City	NV	USA
Las Vegas	NV	USA
Las Vegas	NV	USA
Las Vegas	NV	USA
	NV	USA
Bergen	NY	USA
Amawalk	NY	USA
Ballston Spa	NY	USA
Berryville	NY	USA
Bronxville	NY	USA
Bronxville	NY	USA

Brooklyn	NY	USA
Brooklyn	NY	USA
Brooklyn	NY	USA
Brooklyn	NY	USA
Buffalo	NY	USA
Buffalo	NY	USA
Buffalo	NY	USA
Burnt Hills	NY	USA
Canton	NY	USA
Cuba	NY	USA
Cuba	NY	USA
Delmar	NY	USA
Deposit	NY	USA
Dix Hills	NY	USA
Durham	NY	USA
East Islip	NY	USA
Elmira	NY	USA
Geneva	NY	USA
Geneva	NY	USA
Hempstead	NY	USA
Hempstead	NY	USA
Lindenhurst	NY	USA
Mount Kisco	NY	USA

New Rochelle	NY	USA
New York	NY	USA
New York	NY	USA
New York	NY	USA
New York	NY	USA
New York	NY	USA
New York	NY	USA
New York	NY	USA
New York	NY	USA
New York	NY	USA
New York	NY	USA
New York	NY	USA
New York	NY	USA
New York	NY	USA
New York	NY	USA
New York City	NY	USA
NY	NY	USA
Oceanside	NY	USA
Orange/Sullivan Counties	NY	USA
Owega	NY	USA
Penfield	NY	USA
Poughkeepsie	NY	USA
Poughkeepsie	NY	USA

Poughkeepsie	NY	USA
Rochester	NY	USA
Rochester	NY	USA
Rochester	NY	USA
Rockville Centre	NY	USA
Rotterdam	NY	USA
Saratoga Springs	NY	USA
Selden	NY	USA
Staten Island	NY	USA
Stony Brook	NY	USA
Syracuse	NY	USA
Syracuse	NY	USA
The Bronx	NY	USA
The Bronx	NY	USA
Utica	NY	USA
Utica	NY	USA
West Falls	NY	USA
	NY	USA
Akron	OH	USA
Akron	OH	USA
Akron	OH	USA
Athens	OH	USA

Bexley	OH	USA
Cardington	OH	USA
Cardington	OH	USA
Cincinnati	OH	USA
Cincinnati	OH	USA
Citi	OH	USA
Cleveland	OH	USA
Cleveland	OH	USA
Cleveland Heights	OH	USA
Columbus	OH	USA
Columbus	OH	USA
Columbus	OH	USA
Dayton	OH	USA
Dayton	OH	USA
Dayton	OH	USA
Dayton	OH	USA
Dayton	OH	USA
Kent	OH	USA
Kent	OH	USA
Kent	OH	USA
Medina	OH	USA
North Canton	OH	USA
North Canton	OH	USA

North Canton	OH	USA
Oberlin	OH	USA
Oxford	OH	USA
Parma Heights	OH	USA
Piqua	OH	USA
Southeastern	OH	USA
Springfield	OH	USA
Toledo	OH	USA
Toledo	OH	USA
Toledo	OH	USA
Toledo	OH	USA
Wooster	OH	USA
Wright-Patterson Air Force Base	OH	USA
Yellow Springs	OH	USA
Yellow Springs	OH	USA
Del City	OK	USA
Muskogee	OK	USA
Norman	OK	USA
Norman	OK	USA
Sapulpa	OK	USA
Stillwater	OK	USA
Tulsa	OK	USA

Bend	OR	USA
Eugene	OR	USA
Laurel	OR	USA
Portland	OR	USA
Portland	OR	USA
Portland	OR	USA
Portland	OR	USA
Portland	OR	USA
Portland	OR	USA
Roseberry	OR	USA
Salem	OR	USA
Trail	OR	USA
Tualatin	OR	USA
Tualatin	OR	USA
Annville	PA	USA
Boothwyn	PA	USA
Bridgeville	PA	USA
Bristol	PA	USA
Bryn Mawr	PA	USA
Bryn Mawr	PA	USA
Bryn Mawr	PA	USA
Dallas	PA	USA
East Stroudsburg	PA	USA

Erie	PA	USA
Gettysburg	PA	USA
Harrisburg	PA	USA
Huntingdon Valley	PA	USA
Indiana	PA	USA
Indiana	PA	USA
Kennett Square	PA	USA
Kennette Square	PA	USA
Lancaster	PA	USA
Mansfield	PA	USA
Millersville	PA	USA
Newell	PA	USA
Oxford	PA	USA
Philadelphia	PA	USA
Philadelphia	PA	USA
Philadelphia	PA	USA
Philadelphia	PA	USA
Philadelphia	PA	USA
Philadelphia	PA	USA
Philadelphia	PA	USA
Philadelphia	PA	USA
Philadelphia	PA	USA

Philadelphia	PA	USA
Pittsburg	PA	USA
Pittsburg	PA	USA
Pittsburg	PA	USA
Pittsburg	PA	USA
Pittsburg	PA	USA
Pittsburgh	PA	USA
Scranton	PA	USA
Shippensburg	PA	USA
St. Mary's	PA	USA
Swissvale	PA	USA
Venango City	PA	USA
Waynesburg	PA	USA
West Chester	PA	USA
Wyomissing	PA	USA
Greenville	RI	USA
Providence	RI	USA
Providence	RI	USA
Schuyler	RI	USA
Saunderstown	RI	USA
Warren	RI	USA
Chapel High	SC	USA
Clover	SC	USA

Columbia	SC	USA
Dentsville	SC	USA
Frogmore	SC	USA
Garden City	SC	USA
Spartanburg	SC	USA
Spartanburg	SC	USA
Summerville	SC	USA
Aberdeen	SD	USA
Armour	SD	USA
Sioux Falls	SD	USA
Spearfish	SD	USA
Vermillion	SD	USA
Vermillion	SD	USA
Yankton	SD	USA
Yankton	SD	USA
Beersheba Springs	TN	USA
Halls Crossroads	TN	USA
Hendersonville	TN	USA
Knoxville	TN	USA
Morristown	TN	USA
Nashville	TN	USA
Nashville	TN	USA

Paris	TN	USA
Tusculum	TN	USA
Abilene	TX	USA
Arlington	TX	USA
Arlington	TX	USA
Austin	TX	USA
Austin	TX	USA
Austin	TX	USA
Austin	TX	USA
Austin	TX	USA
Austin	TX	USA
Big Spring	TX	USA
Brownsville	TX	USA
Corpus Christi	TX	USA
Dallas	TX	USA
Dallas	TX	USA
Dallas	TX	USA
Dallas	TX	USA
Fort Worth	TX	USA
Houston	TX	USA
Houston	TX	USA
Houston	TX	USA
Lubbock	TX	USA

McAllen	TX	USA
Mesquite	TX	USA
Mesquite	TX	USA
Morristown	TX	USA
Nacogdoches	TX	USA
Richardson	TX	USA
Roanoke	TX	USA
San Antonio	TX	USA
San Marcos	TX	USA
Steers	TX	USA
Texas City	TX	USA
Texas City	TX	USA
Tyler	TX	USA
Tyler	TX	USA
Willis	TX	USA
Willis	TX	USA
Provo	UT	USA
Salt Lake City	UT	USA
Salt Lake City	UT	USA
Salt Lake County	UT	USA
Sandy	UT	USA
	UT	USA
Alexandria	VA	USA

Annandale	VA	USA
Arlington	VA	USA
Arlington	VA	USA
Charlottesville	VA	USA
Charlottesville	VA	USA
Charlottesville	VA	USA
Fairfax	VA	USA
Fairfax	VA	USA
Fairfax	VA	USA
Locust Grove	VA	USA
Richmond	VA	USA
Richmond	VA	USA
Virginia Beach	VA	USA
Williamsburg	VA	USA
Castleton	VT	USA
Middlebury	VT	USA
Richmond	VT	USA
Bellevue	WA	USA
Bellingham	WA	USA
Bellingham	WA	USA
Bellingham	WA	USA
Bellingham	WA	USA
Bellingham	WA	USA

Cheney	WA	USA
Clinton	WA	USA
Ellensburg	WA	USA
Ellensburg	WA	USA
Ellensburg	WA	USA
Ferndale	WA	USA
Indianola	WA	USA
Index	WA	USA
Lacy	WA	USA
Liberty Lake	WA	USA
Mt. Vernon	WA	USA
Olympia	WA	USA
Olympia	WA	USA
Olympia	WA	USA
Olympia	WA	USA
Olympia	WA	USA
Poulsbo	WA	USA
Pullman	WA	USA
Pullman	WA	USA
Pullman	WA	USA
Pullman	WA	USA
Puyallup	WA	USA
Renton	WA	USA

Sammamish	WA	USA
Seattle	WA	USA
Seattle	WA	USA
Seattle	WA	USA
Seattle	WA	USA
Seattle	WA	USA
Seattle	WA	USA
Seattle	WA	USA
Seattle	WA	USA
Sequin	WA	USA
Skagit Valley	WA	USA
Snoqualmie	WA	USA
Snoqualmie	WA	USA
Spokane	WA	USA
Tacoma	WA	USA
Tacoma	WA	USA
Vancouver	WA	USA
Vancouver	WA	USA
Altoona	WI	USA
Appleton	WI	USA
Bloomer	WI	USA
Chippewa Falls	WI	USA
Chippewa Falls	WI	USA

Colfax	WI	USA
Eau Claire	WI	USA
Eau Claire	WI	USA
Eau Claire	WI	USA
Eau Claire	WI	USA
Eau Claire	WI	USA
Elk Mound	WI	USA
Elkhorn	WI	USA
Fitchburg	WI	USA
Fitchburg	WI	USA
Franklin	WI	USA
Gilman	WI	USA
Green Bay	WI	USA
Hartland	WI	USA
Janesville	WI	USA
La Crosse	WI	USA
Lancaster	WI	USA
Lancaster	WI	USA
Madison	WI	USA
Madison	WI	USA
Madison	WI	USA
Madison	WI	USA
Madison	WI	USA

Madison	WI	USA
Madison	WI	USA
Madison	WI	USA
Madison	WI	USA
Madison	WI	USA
Maple	WI	USA
Menomonie	WI	USA
Menomonie	WI	USA
Milwaukee	WI	USA
Milwaukee	WI	USA
Milwaukee	WI	USA
Milwaukee	WI	USA
Milwaukee	WI	USA
Oshkosh	WI	USA
Platteville	WI	USA
Portage	WI	USA
Racine	WI	USA
Racine	WI	USA
Stevens Point	WI	USA
Stevens Point	WI	USA
Superior	WI	USA
Thorp	WI	USA
Verona	WI	USA

Waukesha	WI	USA
Waukesha	WI	USA
Wausau	WI	USA
Westfield	WI	USA
Fairmont	WV	USA
Huntington	WV	USA
Huntington	WV	USA
Meadow Bridge	WV	USA
Morgantown	WV	USA
Casper	WY	USA
Dayton	WY	USA
Caracas		Venezuela

In Closing...............

In the nearly four years since I started this project much has happened. The last four years of the Trump Administration have shined a direct light on how quickly things can and do change. The focus of my article and this book was to show younger women the history of their rights so that they could become aware and also to become watchful. Little did I know how much things would change in this short time period.

Many groups of people with lots of different names, mainly white supremists, have made their beliefs known and are ready to fight for them. One belief that they have publicly stated is that women having equal rights is not part of the plan. They seem to have gained traction under the last administration, at the least they have felt free to come out publicly and state their beliefs. On January 6th of this new year, 2021, thousands of these people violently stormed and breached the U.S. Capitol in Washington D.C. They claimed, again publicly, that the election was stolen and they will fight to the death to reclaim it for Donald J. Trump. Many people were seriously injured, five+ people died, and there was extensive damage to the Capitol. Rumors of inside help, hired and elected, aided and abetted this siege to stop Congress's certification of the electoral votes. It was interrupted, but after hours of seclusion, they reconvened and finished their job to certify the votes for Joseph Biden. Right now the DC area is on lockdown and tens of thousands of National Guard members are on the grounds preparing to protect the Inauguration of Biden on January 20th. The protesters have made it clear they will be back and be armed.

No one in the world thought anything like this could ever happen in this country. We are in the middle of a serious pandemic with more than 500,000 Americans dead from Covid 19 and it isn't over.

We now have an incoming president who has different beliefs. But the fact remains that there are people out there, in great numbers, who want to change that. These next four years will seem, I hope, much more normal, but the last four years were dangerous for women and now that we have seen how fragile rights can be, we need to be more vigilant than ever.

So as I said nearly four years ago, "please don't be complacent and too comfortable with your life. Be aware of what has happened over the years, decades and literally centuries, to get you here. Many people have died fighting for equal rights for themselves and others. Women fought and died here and abroad. People march to make other people aware; pay attention, please. *It is all I ask, lest you lose it all. Lest we all lose it all.*"

Thanks for reading,

Sharon Weeks

End Notes

Chapter I

1 https://www.biography.com/us-first-lady/abigail-adams

2 https://biography.com/activist/susan-b-anthony

3 https://biography.com/scientist/elizabeth-blackwell

4 https://biography.com/activist/lucy-stone

5 https://biography.com/activist/victoria-woodhull

6 https://biography.com/activist/jane-addams

7 https://biography.com/activist/alice-paul

8 https://www.biography.com/news/famous-womens-rights-activists/maud-wood-park

9 https://www.biography.com/news/famous-womens-rights-activists/mary-mcleod-bethune

10 https://www.biography.com/news/famous-womens-rights-activists/rose-schneiderman

[11]https://www.biography.com/us-first-lady/Eleanor-roosevelt

[12]https://www. biography.com/Margaret-sanger

[13] http://www.nps.gov/article/african-american-women-and-thenineteenthamendment.htm

[14] http://www.gloriasteinem.com/about

[15]https://en.wikipedia.org/wiki/Betty_Friedan

[16] https://www.history.com/topics/black-history/angela-davis

[17] https://en.wikipedia.org/wiki/Hillary_Clinton

[18] https://www.history.com/topics/womens-history/ruth-bader-ginsburg

[19] Posted by Ken Kleinman- on Facebook

[19]https://www.biography.com/people/groups/womens-rights activists

Chapter V

[20] L.A. Times

[21] *The L.A. Times*

[22] https://www.pbs.org/independentlens/blog/unwanted-sterilization-and-eugenics-programs-in-the-united-states/

[23] https://www.who.int/news-room/fact-sheets/detail/female-genital-mutilation

Chapter VI

[24] https://en.wikipedia.org/wiki/Matthew_Shepard

[25] https://www.britannica.com/event/Stonewall-riotse
Editors of Encyclopaedia Britannica

[26] https://www.history.com/topics/gay-rights/the-stonewall-riots

[27]https://www.usatoday.com/story/news/nation/2020/02/11/lgbtq-equality-map-report-shows-advances-challenges-2010-2020/4667911002'

Chapter VII

[28]https://www.dallasnews.com/news/education/2018/11/16/texas-history-curriculum-hillary-clintonand-alamo-heroes-are-in-oprah-s-out/

[29] https://www.nybooks.com/articles/2012/06/21/how-texas-inflicts-bad-textbooks-on-us

Chapter VIII

[30]https://en.wikipedia.org/wiki/Triangle_Shirtwaist_Factory_fire

[31]https://www.britannica.com/event/Triangle-shirtwaist-factory-fire

General Comments

[32] https://mirandagatewood.wwordpress.com/east-end-fringe-festival

[33] https://mirandagatewood.

About the Author

Sharon Weeks is a retired Purchasing Agent/Budget Coordinator from the Chippewa Falls Area Unified School District and is still a member of the Wisconsin Association of Public Procurement where she held all four officer positions.

One of the founding members of the Valley Art Association, she is also a member of the Valley Art Gallery & Gifts in Chippewa Falls along with eleven other women. As a photographer, she has her work at the Gallery and on her website: www.collectionsbysharlow.com. She has also had her work shown at many area galleries/art venues.

What Young Women May Not Know is her first published work beyond newspaper articles/letters. When the article was printed in 2017, the response was overwhelming as it went viral and she received over 4,000 comments on it. They were all printed out and sat in a file in her office until she decided she had to share this information, positive and negative. There were too many to include, so 500+ were chosen to represent the bulk of comments received.

These comments included subjects that she was not fully aware of and the decision was made to put all in book format. Also to expand the details that were not included in the original article because of space limitations.

Besides the comments, she was contact by several people asking for permission to use the article. A group from New

York City, www.womenyoushouldknow.com posted it on their website among others.

She then got a call from Debbie Sleven of Long Island asking permission to use her article in "The 'Future is Female' Festival" by the East End Fringe Festival 'Theater on the Edge' at the Dark Horse Restaurant in Riverhead, N.Y. That was followed by an invitation to attend the event. She accepted and will be forever grateful for the invitation, the wonderful program response, and the whole delightful experience.

She can be contacted at shaweeks@charter.net

Made in the USA
Columbia, SC
30 March 2021